PASTOR DE'RAIN F. IRVIN

Signature Author

IN HIS
PRESENCE

Totally Transformed!

WITH GOD, ALL THINGS ARE POSSIBLE

Disclaimer

The content of this book is designed to educate and entertain the reader. It does not guarantee that the reader will become successful using the methods outlined herein. The author/publisher is not liable or responsible for any loss or damage caused or alleged to be caused, directly or indirectly, by the content of this book.

ISBN: 9798346998273

DEDICATION

To my beloved mother, Noreen A. Gilliam, whose unwavering faith and boundless love inspire me daily. Your Spirit lives on in our hearts, guiding us through life's challenges and reminding us of the beauty of being In HIS Presence. This book is for you and a testament to the legacy of love you have created in our family.

To my fellow authors, thank you for sharing your voices and experiences in this anthology. Your courage and authenticity inspire us to deepen our faith and uplift others on their journeys.

And to our readers, may this collection uplift you and remind you of the profound truth that you, too, can find strength and purpose in your connection with the Divine. We pray that your time spent with these words inspires you to seek your own moments in His presence.

This is a REMINDER ...

This is Your Life; You have the POWER.
to TAKE Authority and be Transformed...

IN HIS PRESENCE
IN YOUR LIFE | CAREER | BUSINESS

IN HIS PRESENCE

Unleash Your **UNLIMITED** Potential!

Jesus looked at them and said, "With man, this is impossible, but with God, ALL things are possible!"
Matthew 19:26 (ESV)

YOU GOT THIS! BECAUSE HE'S GOT YOU!

Totally Transformed!

CONTENTS

FOREWORD

In a world often overshadowed by confusion and despair, "In HIS Presence" shines as a beacon of hope and transformation. This anthology invites readers to witness the profound power of God to change lives through the simple yet profound act of spending time in his presence. The stories within these pages are raw and transparent, offering heartfelt testimonies from believers who have experienced the life-altering grace of God firsthand.

I have had the privilege of knowing Marissa, the visionary author and anthologist behind this remarkable collection, for over two decades. Her unwavering faith and deep commitment to walking alongside God serve as a testament to her authenticity. Marissa doesn't just speak about the goodness of God —she embodies it. Her passion for sharing the transformative stories of others is truly inspiring, and it is an honor to witness her vision come to life through this project.

Originally conceived as part of a six-book series, this first volume is a heartfelt tribute to her late mother, Noreen A. Gilliam. I can only imagine the pride and joy Noreen feels as she watches her daughter fulfill this dream, knowing that these powerful testimonies will touch countless lives.

In these pages, you will find not only stories of struggle and healing but also a reminder of the identity and purpose that can be found in His presence. May these words encourage you to seek a deeper relationship with God and to embrace the transformation that comes from resting in His love.

Welcome to this journey of faith, healing, and renewal. May you be blessed as you read and reflect on the testimonies shared within.

Easter Frazier

ACKNOWLEDGEMENT

As I reflect on the journey that led to the creation of *In HIS Presence*, I am grateful to the many individuals who have supported and inspired me along the way.

First and foremost, I extend my heartfelt thanks to my mother, Noreen A. Gilliam. Your love, wisdom, and unwavering faith continue to be a guiding light in my life. This book is a tribute to you and your legacy in our hearts.

To my siblings, thank you for sharing this sacred journey with me. Your strength and support have been invaluable as we navigated the challenges of loss and embraced the beauty of our shared memories.

I am deeply grateful to all the contributors to this anthology. Your willingness to share your stories and insights adds depth and richness to this work. Together, we create a tapestry of faith demonstrating the power of being In HIS Presence.

Thank you to my friends and mentors who have encouraged, challenged, and walked alongside me in this journey. Your belief in my calling has fueled my passion to share this message with the world.

Finally, I want to express my gratitude to my Heavenly Father. Your love and guidance empower me to pursue this mission, and I am eternally thankful for your constant presence in my life.

May this book inspire others to seek their own connection with the Divine, finding peace and purpose in every moment spent In HIS Presence.

INTRODUCTION

As a public speaker and leader, I often encounter a common question: "How do you do all that you do?" If I were to share it fully, the truth lies in my deep and personal relationship with my Heavenly Father. This constant pursuit of being In HIS Presence empowers me each day.

In HIS Presence is not just a book; it is the first volume in a six-book series titled *Words to Inspire You*, dedicated to the memory of my beloved mother, Noreen A. Gilliam. Her Spirit and wisdom continue to guide me, reminding me of the strength found in faith and the power of connection with the Divine. Last year, the Lord inspired me to expand this journey. I felt a calling to invite other believers to share their own truths and experiences, transforming this single-author book into an anthology highlighting the collective voices of those who also find strength in being In HIS Presence. This collaboration serves as a testament to the transformative power of faith, illustrating that we can all achieve our purpose through our connection with God.

Through the stories and insights shared in this volume, we hope to encourage and uplift one another, demonstrating that no matter the challenges we face, spending time in His presence equips us to fulfill our calling. We pray that our words inspire you, just as my mother's Spirit continues to inspire me, guiding us all to a deeper understanding of love, resilience, and faith. Join us on this journey, and may you find your own truth in the sacred moments spent In HIS Presence.

Marissa L. Bloedoorn

Totally Transformed

"There is no fear in love, but perfect love drives out fear, because fear expects punishment. The person who is afraid has not been made perfect in love."
— 1 John 4:18 (NIV)

It's YOUR Life, TAKE Center Stage & OWN It!

MARISSA L. BLOEDOORN

IN HIS PRESENCE

Totally Transformed

All Fear is Gone

IN HIS PRESENCE

By: Marissa L. Bloedoorn, M.S.C., DTM

"There is no fear in love, but perfect love drives out fear because fear expects punishment. The person who is afraid has not been made perfect in love." — 1 John 4:18 (NIV)

In our journey through life, fear often casts a long shadow over our aspirations and dreams. It whispers doubts and insecurities, urging us to retreat into our comfort zones. Yet, Scripture reminds us that perfect love—God's love—can dispel that fear. This ideal love is not just an abstract concept but a living, breathing reality found in His presence.

When we cultivate a close relationship with our Heavenly Father, we experience love in its most accurate form. It reassures us, comforts us, and strengthens us. Fear may arise, but it is rendered powerless in the light of His perfect love. We understand that our worth is not contingent upon our circumstances or accomplishments but rooted in His unwavering affection for us.

As Psalm 138:8 proclaims, **"The Lord will perfect that which concerns me."** This promise is a beautiful reminder that God is intimately involved in every aspect of our lives. He actively works to refine and shape us, molding our fears into faith and our doubts into hope. In His presence, we find the assurance that we are never alone; we are cherished, and our journey has a purpose.

When we face uncertainty, we can lean on Philippians 4:13: **"I can do all things through Christ who strengthens me."** This verse encapsulates the essence of living a fulfilled life—recognizing that our strength does not come from ourselves but from Christ. In Him, we are empowered to overcome obstacles, to step beyond our fears, and to pursue the calling He has placed on our hearts.

To navigate this journey successfully, we need divine guidance. **"For I know the plans I have for you,"** declares the Lord in Jeremiah 29:11. He has crafted a unique path for each of us, filled with hope and purpose. When we lack clarity or direction, we can turn to the Holy Spirit, our Teacher. He is ever-present to illuminate our path, offering wisdom and discernment that can only be found in His presence.

"You will seek Me and find Me when you seek Me with all your heart." — Jeremiah 29:13 (NIV) This verse invites us into a deeper relationship with God. When we earnestly seek Him, we can rest assured that we will encounter His presence, where our fears begin to dissolve.

In addition, Psalm 16:11 tells us, **"You make known to me the path of life; in Your presence, there is fullness of joy; at Your right hand are pleasures forevermore."** Here, we find the assurance that joy and fulfillment are not just distant dreams, but realities experienced in His presence.

We discover the answers we seek through spending time in HIS Presence. We can pour out our hearts, share our fears, and ask for guidance. In those moments of communion, we receive clarity and peace, knowing we are aligned with His will.

As you reflect on this chapter, consider the areas where fear may be holding you back. Invite God's perfect love into those spaces. Acknowledge His promise to perfect that which concerns you and lean on the strength He provides through Christ. Allow the Holy Spirit to guide you, granting you the wisdom to navigate life's challenges.

Fear transforms into faith, doubt into confidence, and isolation into belonging in His presence. **"The Lord is my light and my salvation; whom shall I fear?"** — Psalm 27:1 (ESV). Embrace the journey ahead, knowing you are being perfected in love with every step taken in faith.

As you dwell in His presence, you will uncover the beautiful truth: you are equipped to fulfill your purpose and live life to the fullest.

Get & Stay Connected @

FB: @marissa.bloedoorn
LI: @marissa-bloedoorn-m-sc-dtm-213864118/
IG: @ownitmagazineandpublishing
X: @TCSwithMARISSA

ABOUT THE ANTHOLOGIST

Marissa L. Bloedoorn

CEO TCS Consulting LLC.
CEO "OWN It!" Magazine & Publishing LLC.
Editor in Chief of "Own It!" Magazine
Master DISC Behavior Analyst,
Certified Executive Leadership Coach
Keynote Speaker | Best Seller | Visionary.

Marissa Bloedoorn is the CEO of TCS Consulting. She has a BS degree in psychology and an MS in industrial-organizational (I-O) psychology. To further her experience, expertise, and education, she is currently enrolled in a doctoral program to complete her PhD in I-O psychology. She recently resigned from her position at Princeton University to run her business full-time. Possessing a diverse background in corporate management and business development, Marissa has been empowering women to think outside the box for over twenty years. Her innovative ideas and methods of discipline have been the key to her success in guiding others to reach beyond their limitations to maximize their performance and potential to succeed.

Marissa's fire and passion for life are infectious, and her youthful flair enables her influence to span generations. Marissa's current initiatives include her non-profit organization, Bridging the Gap (BTG), which strategizes for student success. BTG's mission is to give options to young people through leadership development, build self-confidence through training, and improve public speaking through Toastmasters International.

BTG restores hope to assure students that success is within their reach. The leadership academy is projected to launch in 2020 - 2021. Marissa's published work includes "Take Center Stage."

This is your life. Own it! "The Ultimate Leadership Style," We Are All Leaders, "Maintain Your Superhero Status: A Real Parent's Perspective," and "Sweetheart, Before I Say I Do," her perspective on intimate relationships, today's dating culture, and selecting your partner for life.

Her work also appears in "Words to Inspire You," 6 six-volume motivational and inspirational book series.

And be Ye Transformed

Psalm 16:11 - "You make known to me the path of life; in your presence there is fullness of joy; at your right hand are pleasures forevermore."

APOSTLE CASSANDRA RAINEY

IN HIS PRESENCE

Totally Transformed

AND I WILL GIVE YOU REST

The Comforting Invitation from Jesus

By: Prophetess Cassandra Rainey

"Come to me, all of you who are weary and carry heavy burdens, and I will give you rest."
(Matthew 11:28, NLT)

This verse is a comforting invitation from Jesus, offering consolation and rest to those struggling or overwhelmed. This scripture provided hope and encouragement when I faced some challenging times. I recognized that God was extending an open invitation to come into His presence and share with Him the things that were causing me so much heaviness. This open invitation also assured me that God wanted me in His presence and wanted to help me with the things that concerned me. It is a "Big deal" to think God called me to converse with Him. Do you realize how much God loves you and desires to share in every detail of your life? Do you know that He loves to hear from you?

The phrase "in His presence" typically refers to being in the presence of God or experiencing His closeness. I chose the above scripture because I believe that in the presence of the Lord, you will experience joy, guidance, rest, and a sense of closeness. These feelings encourage me to seek God's presence and trust in His constant companionship and support. My choosing to be in God's presence has helped me to find peace, comfort, and reassurance. In other words, I was provided with what I needed during uncertainty, troubled times, or stressful circumstances. There is no better place to be than being in the presence of the Lord. In the Lord's presence, I discovered His warmness and knew He cared about my well-being.

Experiencing God's presence helped me find direction in my life, make important decisions, and understand my purpose and the path that the Lord had assigned my life. No longer would I be walking around, confused and not knowing what God required of me. Being in God's presence can inspire you to grow spiritually and develop virtues such as compassion, humility, and forgiveness. These are virtues that helped me to transform and grow. Feeling God's presence often comes with a sense of being loved and accepted unconditionally. And who would not want to feel that type of love? To understand what "in His presence" means, you must accept the invitation extended by Jesus to learn what it truly means. Once you meet with the Lord, reflect on your experiences, beliefs, and feelings. Consider moments when you have felt a deep sense of the divine and how those moments have impacted your life.

God has a plan and purpose for your life. You will find it only through a relationship with Him. No one travels through life without experiencing a heavy burden. And how to lighten it by accepting His invitation to come into His presence. Follow the example of Mary in the book of Luke 10:38-42

As Jesus and the disciples continued to Jerusalem, they came to a village where Martha welcomed him into her home. Her sister, Mary, sat at the Lord's feet, listening to what he taught. But Martha was distracted by the big dinner she was preparing. She came to Jesus and said,

"Lord, doesn't it seem unfair that my sister just sits here while I do all the work? Tell her to come and help me."

But the Lord said, "My dear Martha, you are worried and upset over all these details! There is only one thing worth being concerned about. Mary has discovered it; it will not be taken away from her." One can read how much Jesus loved that Mary would stop everything to sit in His presence.

The Prophetic Influence,
Prophetess Cassandra Rainey

Get & Stay Connected @

Website: www.crministriesglobal.com;
LinkedIn: Cassandra Rainey
Facebook: Ap Cassandra Rainey
Instagram its_gone_happen_in_prayer
TikTok: thepropheticinfluencer@28
Facebook Group: A New Day of
Breakthrough Global Outreach Prayer Ministry

ABOUT THE AUTHOR

Apostle Cassandra Rainey

THE PROPHETIC INFLUENCER, PRAYER WARRIOR,
INTERCESSOR, AUTHOR, LICENSED LIFE INSURANCE
AGENT (GA), ENTREPRENEUR AND CEO/FOUNDER OF
CASSANDRA RAINEY GLOBAL MINISTRIES.

She has been in Ministry for over 20 years, beginning in the Crisp County Detention Center jail, where she had the opportunity to pray, minister, teach, and encourage women to become all that God has destined them to become. Although she once ran from the call, she fully embraces it with power and passion that continues to fuel her purpose.

Cassandra Rainey Global Ministries was birthed in 2017 and has been instrumental ever since in touching the lives of many witnessing on the streets/outreach, Bible Study, Revivals, conferences, or ministering in the church. Her areas of focus are Prayer, Evangelism, Breakthrough, and Empowerment. Radical, bold, tenacious kingdom builder, glory carrier, and atmosphere shifter whose greatest desire is to impact everyone she encounters significantly. Daily bringing both men and women together via prayer conference call and A New Day of Breakthrough: 4th Prayer Watch, Facebook Live 5 am, where she inspires, encourages, empowers, as well as interceding on behalf of families, ministries, leaders, cities, states, communities, and nations for salvation, healing, peace, strength, and deliverance.

Prophetess Cassandra states that she is excited about the birth of the first of her many books, *No More Suffering in*

Silence, Let Go and Let God. Which she firmly believes will be a catalyst to push and bring about a significant change in the lives of others. Her continual prayer is that she is a vessel fit for the Master's use while continuing to aim toward a "spirit of excellence." As she continues her journey to destiny, Prophetess Cassandra firmly believes that she is destined for greatness no matter what the enemy sends her way.

And be Ye Transformed...

Psalm 27:4 - "One thing have I asked of the Lord, that will I seek after: that I may dwell in the house of the Lord all the days of my life, to gaze upon the beauty of the Lord and to inquire in his temple."

COACH RAYMOND COLSTON

IN HIS PRESENCE

Totally Transformed

STANDING TALL IN A SHRINKING ROOM

Believing and Trusting God When Things Don't Look Like You Want Them To

By: Coach Raymond Colston

FAITH appears 2,082 times across the most widely read versions of the Bible. Yet, FAITH often seems fragile, fleeting—something many struggle to hold onto consistently. While FAITH is defined biblically as "the substance of things hoped for, the evidence of things not seen," many believers only reach for FAITH in desperation. But even in our inconsistencies, God remains unshakably faithful. God still stands true to His promises as we wrestle with doubt, frustration, and impatience when our prayers go unanswered. At the heart of FAITH is the belief that Christ died and rose again, even though none of us were there to witness it.

This FAITH anchors our love for God and assures us that God has always been and will always be faithful to us, no matter who we once were or what we've been through. We may fall short daily, but we still have direct access to the One who supplies all our needs. The beauty of FAITH lies in knowing that God will fulfill His promises—whether others believe in them or not. Hebrews 11:13 tells us, "Each one of these people of FAITH died not yet having in hand what was promised, but still believing." Moses, for example, never saw the Promised Land, yet he trusted

God enough to follow Him, knowing that something greater was coming.

He accepted that his role might be a small part of a larger story. We must understand that our FAITH calls us firm, even when the world doesn't believe. When things seem bleak and obstacles overwhelming, we must trust that God will make a way. Many have faced situations that should have destroyed us, but God's hand kept us. When doubt creeps in—when the naysayers, the doubters, and the skeptics tell us to give up—we must resist the urge to listen.

We must tune our hearts to God's voice, which tells us to rise and keep moving forward. That same voice tells you to stand up when the pressure feels unbearable, the task seems impossible, and when the world's weight presses down on you. When thoughts of giving up or even suicide whisper in the back of your mind, remember God's voice saying, "Stand up; I am here." My passion for youth drives me forward because I know that God has placed me here for a purpose. Even on days when I'm too sore to walk, too frustrated to push on, or too tired to continue,

I hear God whisper, "Stand up and keep going." The promise may not come in my lifetime, but I know the next generation will inherit a better world because of my FAITH. That's why I stand tall each day. I get up and keep moving because I know someone else's future depends on my perseverance. Remember this: someone is counting on you to keep moving forward. God has assigned souls to each of us, people we are meant to lead to Him.

So, when you feel like quitting, think of the lives depending on you to rise and stand tall no matter the circumstance because the Kingdom of God needs you to carry on. Journal: How can I stand firm in my FAITH when circumstances around me seem overwhelming, and what steps can I take to trust God's promises even when I don't see immediate results?"

Get & Stay Connected @

https://blinq.me/sT0S8rPB3cObHZ79yZnO

ABOUT THE AUTHOR

Coach Raymond Colston

CEO COACH RAY INSPIRES/MOTIVATIONAL SPEAKER/YOUTH LIFE COACH

Business Vision: Where ACCOUNTABILITY, GRIT, and SUPPORT come together.

Mission: To provide empowering, supportive, and transformative coaching, presentations, and services to allow our youth and communities to become the best and most successful versions of themselves.

Coach Ray is a distinguished figure celebrated for his unwavering commitment to nurturing and empowering the next generation. Having graduated from Norfolk Public Schools, he embarked on a dedicated journey in football coaching, where his ethos of servant Leadership emerged as a cornerstone in shaping young lives for success.

Alongside his role as the Youth Ministry Director at First Baptist Church of South Hill, Coach Ray is also recognized as a powerful motivational speaker fervently dedicated to ensuring the next generation's success.

With a passionate and empathetic coaching approach, he utilizes diverse strategies to forge meaningful connections between students, educators, families, and communities, laying the groundwork for their ascent to even greater heights of achievement.

And be Ye Transformed...

Psalm 46:10 - "Be still, and know that I am God. I will be exalted among the nations; I will be exalted in the earth!"

SAKINAH N. FREEMAN

IN HIS PRESENCE

Totally Transformed

BE STILL

By: Sakinah N. Freeman

"Trust in the Lord with all your heart; do not depend on your own understanding.

Seek his will in all you do, and he will show you which path to take".
(Proverbs 3: 5-6 NLT)

For many years, I have done things my way. My way of living without any guidance or relationship with the Lord. I equated church and GOD as "punishment" due to my childhood experiences. As a child, my family would attend church, bible school, after-service programs, and then dinner every Sunday. We were in church all day and couldn't say no as a child. I would have preferred to be at home doing kids' stuff like playing with my dolls, watching my favorite cartoons like Thunder Cats and Scooby-doo, or telling on my two older sisters. Eventually, I realized what I was doing was not working. As an adult, I knew I was missing something. I felt incomplete. One day, my co-worker invited me to attend church. She talked about her fantastic experience and suggested I attend. I realized at that moment that I was subconsciously avoiding" church." After about two months of procrastination, I took the leap of faith and just went. I was welcomed with open arms; everyone appeared happy and friendly. I thought I was in heaven. The sermon was tremendous and life-changing. I felt like I was hit with lightning because I could not describe this new feeling. It was an awkward good feeling. One Wednesday afternoon, I heard God's voice, and he said, "Be Still." I almost fell out of my chair. I asked my co-worker if she had heard anything. She repeatedly said "NO." In this transition, I've learned to be obedient. So, I obeyed the command. I am STILL,

I surrendered to the Lord on July 16th, 2023, and was baptized. Since then, this exhilarating and spiritual experience has continued to live inward and outward in my life. I am at peace and no longer confused about life or my purpose. I have a new lens and am walking on the journey of my true assignment. My life is full of blessings; my career is flourishing, and my goals and dreams are coming to fruition.

God is my father and Creator; he knows me, and now I only seek him through prayer and the Word instead of advice from people. The scripture says," Come to me, all of you who are weary and carry heavy burdens, and I will give you rest. Take my yoke upon you. Let me teach you because I am humble and gentle; you will find rest for your souls. My yoke is an easy bear, and the burden I give you is light. (Matthew 11- 28-30 NLT)

I want to encourage you to form a relationship with GOD; he is waiting for you. Let him into your life, and you will see miracles happen. Seek him and "Be still in the presence of the lord and wait patiently for him to act" (Psalm 37:7 NLT). God will fight for you, "He says. "Be still and know that I am GOD." (Psalm 46:10 NLT).

Sakinah N. Freeman

ABOUT THE AUTHOR

Sakinah N. Freeman

Sakinah N. Freeman is a Social Worker, Certified Grief Counselor, Mental Health Advocate, and Author. Sakinah is one of the co-authors for Joy Comes in the Morning. Sakinah is the mother of 3 adult daughters and enjoys spending time with her three grandchildren.

Email: info@healingheartsmindandsoul.org

And be Ye Transformed...

Psalm 46:10 - "Be still, and know that I am God. I will be exalted among the nations; I will be exalted in the earth!"

BARRY S. RICOMA

IN HIS PRESENCE

Totally Transformed

THE PAST, THE PRESENT, AND THE FUTURE
My Walk In His Presence

By: Barry S. Ricoma

The PAST…

My walk in His presence started out spending five years of my life living with my grandmother in Brooklyn, NY, as my mother went off to build her career in the US Army during the 1970s. Growing up in a Roman Catholic home was filled with strict adherence to Sunday church, prayer, choir practice, and completing First & Second communion, of which I only finished my first. I was young, so I did not fully understand what it meant to be religious and devoted to God's Word. I did what my elders told me to do and followed their examples. When my mother completed her training and I could travel with her, I was exposed to other types of denominations that spread God's Word with varying degrees of interpretation. A bit older at this point, I began to understand (still not entirely) that there were many ways to express and appreciate different interpretations of what it feels like to be in his presence. This understanding forever shaped my relationship with God as I came into my own as a young man.

The PRESENT…

His presence along my journey has served as a beacon of light both during many happy moments in my life as well as during some of the most challenging and heartbreaking tribulations that have to this day left me questioning, at times, my worth as a man, a father, and (when I was one) a husband. I was utterly lost but mostly angry. I was furious at the world for trying to hold me back; at least, that is what I told myself to justify my reasoning and actions moving through life. I was angry at the people whom I trusted with my heart who took me for granted and then later abandoned me when I was no longer of value. Lastly, I was angry at MYSELF for being weak-willed and rejecting His presence in guiding me down a better path. Since then, as I am typing in this continued present, I have experienced renewed faith, inner strength, and recognition of His signs to guide my way. In these recent three years of being in His Presence, I have been blessed with a promising career, have built positive and unbreakable connections with good people, and developed a stronger spiritual character. I found a new purpose through creative writing that has opened and expanded my understanding of his plan for me. I am grateful for His knowledge, patience, and unconditional love!

The FUTURE...

As I turn fifty-two this year, I look towards my unwritten future without fear or anxiety but with optimism, excitement, hope, and love, knowing that His Presence is always with me. AMEN!

I share my testimony for my future with you.

Get & Stay Connected @

Website: www.crministriesglobal.com;

THE BEE AND THE ROSE

By

Barry S. Ricoma

In the desert's expanse, I soar,
Seeking the elusive desert rose,
Like a bee drawn to a flower's core.
Hope and vitality it bestows.

Wings beat with determination's flow,
Barren landscape beneath me lies.
Anticipation, a vibrant glow,
As I embrace the beauty that never dies.

Landing delicately, petals embrace,
In the rose, new hope I trace.

The desert rose symbolizes possibility, echoing a desire to open my heart to new love. My wish for a divine counterpart resonates with the delicate dance between the bee and the rose, a symphony of mutual appreciation and growth promising a flourishing oasis in the arid expanse of my heart.

ABOUT THE AUTHOR

Barry S. Ricoma

Barry's mission and vision are simply to share his love for Travel and the outdoors and hopefully inspire others through examples of both His failures and achievements.

A two-time Best-Selling and International author, Barry S. Ricoma is a native of Brooklyn, New York, a Father to one son (Ryan), and a 21-year Veteran of the Military Armed Forces (US Army). He is currently residing in Hawthorne, Nevada. When not working, Barry engages in his passion for the great outdoors.

Whether cruising the highways on his motorcycle (2018 Harley-Davidson Fat Bob) or enjoying nature to its fullest beauty when camping in the nearby National Forests in California. His thirst for adventure and the desire to experience what life offers on his journey makes him so successful!

GET & STAY CONNECTED @

Email: twowheeledfreedomofficial@gmail.com
Website: https://twowheeledfreedom.com/
FB: https://www.facebook.com/TheWritersBlock.TWF
YouTube:
https://www.youtube.com/@twowheeledfreedom_offici
al InstaGram: Two_Wheeled_Freedom X (Formally Twitter): bsr_2whldfredm

And be Ye Transformed...

James 4:8 - "Draw near to God,
and he will draw near to you."

DR. PETRICE MCKEY-REESE

IN HIS PRESENCE

Totally Transformed

I AM GOD'S CHILD

By: Dr. Petrice McKey-Reese

I said, Ye are God s, and all of you are children of the Most High. —
Psalm 82:6 (NIV)

*You created my inmost being; you knit me together in my mother's
womb. I praise You because I am fearfully and wonderfully made:
your works are wonderful; I know that full well.* **Psalm 139 (NIV)**

In the depths of our identity, we often seek affirmation and
purpose. The Book of Psalms lays a profound foundation for
understanding who we are with God. Psalm 82:6 declares, "I
said, 'You are God s, and all of you are children of the Most
High,'" while Psalm 139 paints a picture of our intricate creation
and intimate relationship with Our Heavenly Father.

From the moment of conception, it is evident in the divine
intention of our Creator. Psalm 139 reminds us that we are
"fearfully and wonderfully made." Each intricacy of our total
being—our thoughts, emotions, the essence of our existence
meticulously crafted by God.

As we ponder the words in Psalm 82:6, we recognize an
undeniable truth: we are not merely creations; we are heirs to
the divine, designed to reflect God's nature in the world. This
dual identity as both human and divine resonates deeply within
us. It urges us to embrace our role as children of the Most High,
imbued with dignity, Authority, and purpose.

Being a child of God carries profound implications and
responsibility. It demonstrates our worth, which is not
contingent upon the opinions of others or the circumstances we

face. In a world that often measures value by achievements or status, God's declaration of our identity stands firm and unshakeable.

Psalm 139 emphasizes that we are known and seen, even in our most vulnerable moments. "When I sit and rise, you perceive my thoughts from afar." This intimate knowledge means that we are never alone. God walks with us, understands our struggles, and celebrates our victories. Our identity as His children shapes our understanding of love, acceptance, and belonging.

The family of God transcends boundaries, cultures, and backgrounds. We are united not by our perfection but by our shared journey as God's children. Psalm 139 reassures us that we belong to a greater narrative, one that is woven with love and grace. As we navigate our lives, we can take comfort in knowing we are part of something much larger than ourselves. Being a child of God involves growing in faith, learning to love, and extending grace to ourselves and others.

The affirmation of being God's child is not just a title but a call to action. It invites us to live fully in the truth of who we are, to embrace our divine heritage, and to engage with the world in a way that reflects our Creator. As we meditate on the truths in Psalm 82:6 and 139, let us step boldly into our identity. We are fearfully and wonderfully made, empowered and loved, called to make a difference as children of the Most High. Embrace this truth, and let it transform how you live, love, and interact with the world around you.

When we are in God's presence as His children, several profound experiences and transformations can occur:

Intimacy and Connectivity - We find a deep intimacy in God's presence. As His children, we can approach Him freely, knowing we are accepted by the beloved. This connection allows us to share our hearts with Him openly, leading to deeper connectivity and honest communication, which leads to true revelation and understanding.

Peace, Hope, and Rest - In God's presence, we often find peace and a restored hope that transcends our circumstances. It's a place where worries fade, and we can rest in His sovereignty. This peace and hope reassure us that we are secure in His care.

Identity Affirmed – Experiencing continuous encounters with God strengthens our identity as His children and heirs. We receive affirmation of our worth and purpose, reminding us that we are valued and loved just as we are.

Transformative Growth - Being in God's presence will lead to personal transformation when we allow it. His holiness challenges us to learn, grow, and refine our character, drawing us closer to the image and likeness of Christ. We may find ourselves inspired to let go of burdens, habits, or fears that hinder our spiritual journey.

Clear Guidance - In the presence of God, we often gain clarity and direction. We may receive wisdom about our paths, decisions, and relationships, helping us navigate life purposefully and confidently.

The Joy that Comes When We Worship - God's presence fills us with joy, prompting us to worship. As His children, we respond with gratitude and praise, celebrating His goodness and faithfulness.

Empowered to Serve - Being in God's presence equips us for service. We are reminded of our calling and the gifts He has bestowed upon us, inspiring us to serve others and share His love.

Community and Belonging
We experience a sense of belonging in God's presence—to Him and the broader family of believers. This community provides

support, encouragement, and a shared mission to reflect His love to the world.

As God's children, being in His presence is a transformative experience. It transforms our hearts, strengthens our faith, and empowers us to live out our purpose, life, and identity more meaningfully. Through our relationship with Our Heavenly Father, we discover the fullness of life He intended for us.

In God's Presence, I find peace
In God's Presence, I find Joy
In God's Presence, I find Liberty

Dr. Petrice M. McKey-Reese

"Too Blessed To Be Stressed"

GET & STAY CONNECTED @

FB: @Dr-PetriceMcKey-ReeseThe Author
IG: Dr.PetriceMcKey-Reese
Website: www.authorpetricemckeyreese.com
Email: mckeyreesepm@yahoo.com

ABOUT THE AUTHOR

Dr. Petrice McKey-Reese

Dr. Petrice M. McKey-Reese is a retired veteran, published Author, certified coach, wife, mother, grandmother, and Child of God. She loves to help people. She was born in New Orleans, LA, to the late Mrs. Theodora R. McKey, the second oldest of four girls. The two men most influential in her life were the men she considers her father who raised me, Herbert Eskinde Jr., and her uncle Darryl McCray. She graduated from L. B. Landry High School in 1983, joined the United States Army in April 1984, and proudly served the military for over 30 years.

I have been Blessed to be featured in three newspaper articles, The Fayetteville Press Newspaper 2nd Edition, September 26th to October 10th, 1994: "McKey, Hooked On The Airborne". Then, The Army Times in December of 2014, "Only African American Female to serve as Rigger Warrant Officer Retires." The last time was in January of 2019 on radio.com, "10 African American Female Service Members Who Have Made History". In March 2018, I was inducted into the United States Army's Women Hall of Fame Foundation. Then, to Culminate the Blessings bestowed upon me in February 2020, I was inducted into the Colonel Thomas R. Cross Parachute Rigger Hall of Fame as the 71st inductee.

I have enjoyed working on two 90-Day Devotionals with 89 other outstanding authors. We made International Best Seller and Best Seller on both of those 90-Day Devotionals titled "Finding Joy in the Journey" and "Finding Joy in the Journey – Vol 2," Presented by Dr. Vernessa Blackwell and A Collaboration of Authors. I completed working on another Devotional and an Affirmation Journal with 364 other outstanding authors. It is titled Joy 365, A Devotional for Joy Restoration and Choose Joy and Affirmation Journal. The Devotional and Affirmation Journal made the #1 Amazon Best Seller and International Best Seller List.

In September 2021, a very good friend of mine, Theresa (Tre) Smith, and I joined forces to establish our Sorority, Zeta Pi Theta Sorority for Military Women Inc., for the betterment of women who serve(d) in the Armed Forces worldwide.

And be Ye Transformed...

Psalm 91:1 - "He who dwells in the secret place of the Most High shall abide under the shadow of the Almighty."

DR. RENATA A. WALTON

IN HIS PRESENCE

Totally Transformed

WASHING FEET:
The Dance of Humility and Servitude

By: Dr. Renata A. Walton

Who on God's green earth would choose feet from all the preferred body parts that one could wash? Simply and profoundly – God did! The Gospel of John (13: 1-17) reveals an awe-inspiring moment when Jesus humbled Himself to wash His disciples' feet at the Last Supper. This act transcends mere symbolism; it embodies the essence of humility and servitude. And so, dear readers, let us embark on a journey to explore the profound beauty of these virtues, often misunderstood yet profoundly transformative.

In the tapestry of the American psyche, humility is often misconstrued as the plight of the weak, an emblem of inadequacy. It can evoke images of subservience and vulnerability. Yet, here lies our initial misunderstanding. Humility, though stemming from the same root as humiliation, is its noble counterpart. Humiliation may bend one towards humility, but the chasm between the two is as vast as heaven and earth. Humility is not a surrender of strength but a manifestation of grace. It beckons us to a place of inner reflection and genuine recognition of our place within the grand design.

Personal trials can be formidable teachers of humility. Moments of humiliation can be jarring awakenings, redirecting us toward the Divine within. Like a well-placed slap that snaps us back to reality, we realize the need for divine correction. Remember the stories of Job, Paul's thorn, Peter's denial, and King Nebuchadnezzar – they all journeyed through humiliation to discover the goldmine of humility and acknowledge God's all-encompassing sovereignty. While the price is steep, the reward is beyond measure – to stand righteous in the presence of the divine.

Now, let us return to the washing of feet. It's more than a physical act; it's a divine dance between humility and servitude. Humility paves the way, and servitude follows closely behind. The pages of history are adorned with the tarnished legacy of servitude, often marred by subjugation and pain. But in the light of God's presence, service becomes a transcendental experience. Observe the life of Jesus, a living testament to service. In every scripture, He serves God and humanity with unwavering dedication. The equation is simple: as we extend ourselves in service, we become a living reflection of Christ, our souls ablaze with divine purpose.

Whether grand or seemingly insignificant, service ignites a transformation within. It is an alchemic process where our ego dissolves, and our hearts expand to embrace the needs of others. Each service rendered is a brushstroke on the canvas of our soul, creating a masterpiece of compassion and grace. By serving, we become conduits of divine love and heaven's benevolence.

The washing of feet is a historical event and a living parable that illustrates the dance of humility and servitude. Humility awakens us to our true essence, while servitude propels us into the realm of divine purpose. Together, they orchestrate a symphony of grace that transforms our lives and those we touch. Let us humbly embrace the call to serve; in doing so, we align our steps with a divine choreography that leaves footprints of love and light for generations.

Dr. Renata A. Watton

GET & STAY CONNECTED @

Email: Rannette439@gmail.com
         drrawenterprise@gmail.com

ABOUT THE AUTHOR

Dr. Renata A. Walton

Dr. Renata A. Walton is a trailblazer and thought leader with over 30 years of experience as an organizational strategist with an acute focus on innovation, training, and communications. Within these impressive three decades, Dr. Walton has cultivated a legacy of empowering high-performing teams to embrace their native genius while fostering a culture of operational excellence. Dr. Walton has consistently demonstrated her visionary prowess in creating enduring and innovative programs and processes in her various professional roles in technology and health sciences. Recognized for her unwavering dedication to progress and expertise, Dr. Walton is a sought-after speaker. She has presented at two prestigious industry conferences, sharing her groundbreaking insights and innovative best practices within pharmaceutical promotional review.

Not content with her professional accomplishments, Dr. Walton pursued her passion and was inspired to establish a youth mentoring program for girls. She conceived and orchestrated the "Tiaras to Crowns" mentoring program. The program focused on providing spiritually grounded real-world skills and practical learning experiences to nurture these young minds and empower compassionate individuals rooted in foundational God ly values. Renata is a dedicated community activist in her hometown. Her commitment led her to the Board of Education in 2010, where she served four years and assumed the mantle of President for a commendable two-year term. During her tenure, the city launched its first 7th through 12th-grade honors high school focused on the arts, technology, and scholarship. Plainfield Academy for the Arts & Advanced Studies (PAAAS) has received national and state recognition and has consistently achieved a 100% graduation rate.

As a consummate learner, Dr. Walton embarked on a transformative doctoral journey, delving into the depths of the Appreciative Inquiry methodology. Her focus was on the innovative concept of reverse mentoring within her organization – a dynamic approach to preparing Millennial knowledge workers for leadership roles. Through rigorous research, she ingeniously crafted a comprehensive framework that equips organizational leaders with the tools and strategies to integrate reverse mentoring, fostering intergenerational knowledge exchange and fortifying the organization's future. Her knowledge and experience also extended to academia, where she guided aspiring scholars through their doctoral journey during two University of Phoenix-sponsored colloquiums.

Dr. Walton is channeling her expertise into writing compelling journal articles, book chapters, and curricula, shedding light on the transformative power of reverse mentoring and the art of appreciative inquiry. Her scholarly efforts have not gone unnoticed, as she was nominated for Dissertation of the Year – a testament to her exceptional academic contributions. She is a published author for *ProQuest LLC* and a scholarly journal, "AI Practitioner." *She* is currently co-authoring a chapter on Leadership entitled: "Futureproofing A Resilient Leadership Pipeline Through Reverse Mentoring," to be included in a professional development book, *Resilience of Multicultural and Multigenerational Leadership and Workplace Experience*, slated for publication in April of 2024.

And be Ye Transformed...

Matthew 18:20 - "For where two or three are gathered in my name, there am I among them."

LEON T. DALES, JR.

IN HIS PRESENCE

Totally Transformed

EVEN WHEN I DIDN'T KNOW HIM...
HE KNEW ME

By: Leon T. Dales, Jr.

Experiencing God profoundly affects my relationships with others, allowing me to embrace a non-judgmental attitude. I am acutely aware of my flaws, which fills my heart with love for my fellow man. I treat everyone respectfully and kindly, regardless of their situation or status. This awareness of God's presence provides comfort and strength, as He has answered my prayers and transformed challenging circumstances into opportunities for growth. My faith in Him remains unwavering, rooted not in what I've read or been told but in the personal experiences that have shaped my understanding of His reality.

From a young age, I witnessed the love of God through my mother, who permanently extended her kindness to others, and through my uncle, the Reverend, who would admonish me to "get right with God." These influences planted seeds of faith in my heart. Throughout my life, I have seen God respond to my prayers, guiding me through the darkest valleys of addiction and despair. When I thought I was at the end, He would tap me on the shoulder, whispering, "I am still here."

In the quiet moments of my day, I feel the warmth of a presence that has walked with me through life's shadows. It's a gentle embrace that reassures me I am not alone.

This presence, a constant light, reshapes my existence and influences how I see and love those around me. It's all too easy to judge or turn away from the struggles of others when wrapped in personal comfort. Yet, as I delve deeper into God's love, I recognize our shared humanity. Each interaction becomes an opportunity to offer kindness and honor our burdens.

My knowledge of God's presence fills me with strength. I have witnessed miraculous answers to my prayers, lifting me from despair and turning my darkest moments into stepping stones toward grace. My faith is forged in the crucible of experience, a testament to the undeniable truth of God's existence. Looking back, I see how the seeds of faith were sown through my mother's loving actions and my uncle's sincere warnings.

I can trace the fingerprints of God throughout my life, even in moments of ignorance about His presence. The struggles with alcohol and drugs felt insurmountable; nights spent in darkness seemed endless. Yet, I would feel that familiar nudge in those moments—a soft reminder that I was cherished and seen. God's presence has been a constant, even when I wandered far. Sometimes, I didn't realize I was being cradled in His arms, but He knew me intimately, guiding me through turbulent waters.

Standing in the light of this awareness, I fully surrender my life at His feet. "Do with me as you wish, Dear Lord," I whisper, my heart open and vulnerable. This profound awareness fuels my relationships, filling my heart with love that invites connection. Each person I meet carries their own stories of struggle, and recognizing this compels me to treat them with dignity and respect. In the grand tapestry of life, we are all woven together, and our love reflects the divine spark within each of us.

As I walk this path, I am reminded that faith is not merely a doctrine but a lived experience, a vibrant testament to love and grace. Even when I didn't know Him, He knew me—every misstep, every tear, every moment of doubt. In this beautiful truth, I find my purpose and the strength to love others without hesitation.

In the tapestry of my life, I've come to understand that I am never truly alone. Even in moments of uncertainty and despair, God's presence envelops me, guiding my steps and illuminating my path. Each day is a reminder that His love is unwavering, a constant companion in my journey.

Even when I didn't know Him, He was there, intricately weaving His grace through every experience. Now, with a heart fully aware of His presence, I embrace the joy of knowing I am His child, cherished and loved. I confidently move forward, trusting that no matter where life leads, I am always held in His embrace, forever secure in His infinite love.

Leon T. Dales, Jr.

GET & STAY CONNECTED @
Facebook: www.facebook.com/leon.dales

ABOUT THE AUTHOR

Leon T. Dales, Jr.

RET. US NAVY & BUSINESS PROFESSIONAL

He has served Philadelphia and the surrounding area for over 20+ years in the home improvement industry, specializing in quality assurance, general contracting, heating and cooling systems, and kitchen and bath full-service remodeling. Leon has contracted with real estate agents, homeowners, and real estate investors to remodel more than 50 homes (complete remodeling projects), more than 100 kitchen and bathroom renovations, and countless remodeling and repair jobs starting from window and door replacements, flooring, heaters, air conditioning, and roof repairs in both residential and commercial properties. His preferred high-end appliances include but are not limited to Kohler, Viking, and American Standard.

He attributes his success to building relationships with his clients, offering fair pricing, and keeping his Word. He never had to advertise a new business, resulting from satisfied customers and word-of-mouth. He is known for his honesty and excellence in quality of service, which distinguishes him from his competitors. That is his reputation on the street and among other professionals in his industry.

Of all the skills he has mastered through his experience as a general contractor, carpentry is his favorite. He loves to build, watch movies, play solitaire, and vintage shopping. He hopes to retire and have his vintage store to collect the things he loves, sell them, and build custom furniture for his customers.

And be Ye Transformed...

Psalm 139:7-10 - "Where shall I go from your Spirit? Or where shall I flee from your presence?"

LAWRENCE STOKES

IN HIS PRESENCE

Totally Transformed

AND THEN IT ALL BECAME CLEAR...

By: Mr. Lawrence Stokes

The philosopher Soren Kierkegaard said, "Life can only be understood backward, but it must be lived forward. This is one of those profound quotes and speaks volumes as it alludes to how we may understand our journey through life, our experiences, and how we have arrived at the place we are right now.

Have you ever taken the time to reflect on your life? Have you ever asked yourself questions about specific periods in your life, those "what-if" questions? Have you ever looked back and tried to pinpoint the exact moment your life changed, that moment that put you on a different path and led you to where you are right now? I'm almost sure we've all had that moment, that experience, that life-changing event that changed our lives, if not forever, but for many years. If you have done that, you may now understand where you are in life, and more will be revealed during your journey.

Over the years, I have reflected on my life many times. I have asked many questions about my journey. I even tried to pinpoint the exact moment when life presented me with different twists and turns. I have asked myself specific "what-if" questions that I would never get a definitive answer. Questions like "Where would I be or who would I be if my mother had not died when I was 8?" Where would

I be or who would I be if my father did not die when I was 18?" Those questions remain unanswered, but I can tell you that certain events that have taken place only made me reflect on a deeper level.

Psalms 16:9 says, "We make our plans, but the Lord determines our steps." I have often heard the quote, "Make your plans in pencil because God has the eraser." Both quotes, although interchangeable, speak volumes and paint a more incredible picture in the grand scheme of the purpose each of us serves in this life and service to each other.

There are appointed places and times we are supposed to be, and our steps are ordered for us to fulfill the will of God to be at those places and at the time we are supposed to be there. God's timing is perfect, and if you look back over your life, you will begin to see that you are exactly where you're supposed to be when you were supposed to be there.

The plans I made for my life may have worked for a short period, but chaos ensued without notice and warning, and I was placed on a different path. Looking back, this was God's will. No matter how devastating, it had to happen. I was supposed to be at an appointed place and time. My plans were obviously in pencil because God quickly erased them to set me on the path I was supposed to be on.

What if I did not listen? I would not have the career I now have; I would not have the seven beautiful grandchildren I now have, and my life may have been more complicated than I could have imagined. God does not make mistakes, and I often tell people that we can listen to God, or he can snatch the rug out from underneath, leaving you no choice but to do as you have been called. You will be where you are supposed to be because that's precisely where he wants you.

Have you ever put a jigsaw puzzle together, and as you are putting the pieces together, you have completed the outline and are now working your way toward completion... You step back to look over your work, and then before actual completion, it all becomes clear.... You can now see what the completed puzzle will look like. This is life. This is when you have looked over your life and reached conclusions about specific parts of your life. Some things may have been revealed to you that gave you an epiphany about your life.

And as that puzzle nears completion.... THEN IT ALL BECAME CLEAR. As with your life, you realize that you are exactly where you are supposed to be. Your steps were ordered. Walk in power!

"We make our plans, but the Lord orders our steps.

Get & Stay Connected @

FB: Lawrence Stokes
IG: LStokes44
X: TheRealLStokes

ABOUT THE AUTHOR

Mr. Lawrence Stokes

Born and raised in Bridgeport, Connecticut, and graduated from Central High School. A retired Navy veteran, Lawrence Stokes has earned his Master of Arts degree in Professional Development with a minor in Counseling from Dallas Baptist University Dallas, Texas.

He holds a Bachelor of Science in Applied Science from the University of North Texas and an associate degree in paralegal from El Centro College Dallas, Texas.

And be Ye Transformed...

1 Chronicles 16:11 - "Seek the Lord and his strength; seek his presence continually!"

ERIN BAER

IN HIS PRESENCE

Totally Transformed

GOD'S UNWAVERING LOVE
And An Envelope

By: Mrs. Erin Baer

God's Unwavering Love and an Envelope
Written by: Erin Baer 3/1/2022

It's around 3 am on March 1st, 2022, and I am awake. I was awakened by not only my cats playing in the night but also the pain that was surrounding my incisions from my surgery. I have been tossing and turning for the past half hour, trying to relax and go back to sleep unsuccessfully. So, here I am as I type my thoughts. As I lay in bed trying to clear my mind, an overwhelming thought rushed calmly through my mind: God's unwavering love. I have always known that God never leaves and is always with me, even if I don't feel his presence around me. But that absence of feeling his nearness solely lies on me. I am the one who turns away, whether it be out of sadness, fear, embarrassment, or feeling undeserving; it's me who turns my back and runs.

The image that comes to my mind is one of me being scared of the dark as a child. Instead of reaching out with my arms wide open, I turn, run to a corner, and hide, consumed by my fears. Instead of turning towards God, I turn away, thinking I can figure it out all alone, knowing I can't.

Amid the storms I face, it's in the turmoil of the winds that I turn to understand rather than go inward to the eye of the storm where I can find peace within all the chaos. I have gotten better at recognizing when the storms are on the horizon, bracing for them, and looking up towards God, asking Him to take my hand rather than turning and running away. But just as a child afraid of the dark and hiding in a corner, hoping the light will be turned on, I sometimes let go of God and cover my eyes, waiting for it to pass.

Yet, God is still there, holding, guiding, and loving me. He never leaves me. His love is truly unwavering. It doesn't matter how often I try to let go, turn away, run away, or deny Him; he is still there for me, whether I deserve it. I probably don't most of the time, but his love again is unwavering and truly unconditional.

I am in the midst of a storm, one of the longest and most unpredictable ones yet of my life, and I realize how hard it can be to trust God, yet when I feel lost the most, it's because I have turned away from the light of his love.
All God is pure light and love, and he shines so brightly that we are blinded when we try to open our eyes to it. It's uncomfortable, so we cover our eyes, turn away, and shield ourselves because something so beautiful seems unreachable amid the darkness we are going through.

I am learning that my eyes will adjust, and my heart can open to the beauty of God's unwavering love. Over time, I can trust him completely. Those words seem so ridiculous even to question *trusting him completely*... He has given me no reason not to, yet my doubts, self-sabotaging thoughts, and fear of letting stand in the way of a beautiful and open relationship with God.

Is it that I don't feel that I deserve it? No, because I truly believe I deserve it. What stops me from fully leaning in and being completely faithful is that I may mess it up. Yet, he reminds me that I can't do anything to lose his love. But how can that be? How do I not disappoint him when I question his plan, ask his presence, and even myself?

When we turn our backs on Him, it hurts Him because it ultimately hurts us. He doesn't want us to feel pain, loss, sadness, exhaustion or depletion. He wants us to feel whole and loved because we are – regardless of what we may face.

My journey of infertility has been arduous in so many ways, and many times, I have questioned my strength in all of it. People continuously tell me I am strong, yet I lost my strength long ago; I am determined. I set goals, and I always accomplish them. Yet, the goal of becoming a mother has been the toughest one I have set my mind on in every way imaginable. I have tried everything to conceive a child, one to carry within my womb, but have come empty-handed every time. I have three angel babies in heaven, and I know God is watching over them. I keep pushing, I keep questioning, and I keep asking why. The answer I always fill in is that God has a plan. I truly believe He does, but why do I keep questioning it? Why am I so eager to know right this minute, and why do I keep looking towards the storm's winds rather than the eye where it's calm, where I KNOW I will find God and have more peace? Because I am afraid of the light, I fear what the truth will reveal, and I fear to step fully in faith.

However, I am getting closer. I have talked with friends

and God for several months about *pushing the envelope* and when it will be too much. But what if the real question isn't about pushing and it's about opening? Maybe the answer has always been there: I have done it wrong. If I have been going the wrong way – questioning God by pushing the envelope- that means I was stubborn, which is a trait I have. It also means I was holding onto that envelope too tightly, afraid of what's inside. And it mostly means that I am scared to let go and have complete faith in God for his plan for me.

I am trying not to beat myself up about "pushing the envelope" regarding my idea of becoming a mother or how that goal would be accomplished. To be honest, I am still struggling.

However, I have been thinking about when it will be enough for several months. When will I know when to stop "pushing the envelope"? But that's as far as I went. I have been asking for a sign from God to let me know that it hasn't been for nothing. The sign is an answer, and what if it's been in my hands all along? What if the answer has been inside the envelope that I have been holding onto so tightly and pushing so hard? What if God has been simply saying, "Release your grip, turn the envelope over, and open it, my child? Let go, and you will see the plans I have for you". Yet, I am that child in the dark, sitting in a corner waiting for someone to turn the light on so I can see when all I need to do is stand up, turn around, and look towards God because he is the light.

I have been so afraid to let go of my envelope, but I need to because it's been exhausting in every way imaginable. Infertility may not have been a part of "my plan," but it is a part of God's plan, and that plan is in the envelope that I hold onto so tightly. I am loosening my grip; I am turning towards God, and I am asking for him to help me with the rest of my infertility journey. As much as I know, I haven't been walking this path alone; he has been by my side. I need to trust him fully and have him carry me through. I need him to be my strength (though I know he has been for some time now), and I need him to help me open the envelope so His plan can be revealed.

I'm scared because I know it won't be what I thought it should be, it won't make sense to me right away, and I probably won't see the beauty within it all. That's where my faith needs to be bigger than my fear.

As I sit and write about the unwavering love of God, I feel more at peace. I think that I am slowly letting go of my stubbornness when it comes to how my "infertility journey" will continue or even end. I also feel a sense of clarity about what conversations I need to have moving forward. I may be tired, but that's okay. Now I know I am not stuck. I just need to figure out the direction that is meant for me.

Sitting in the dark with the only light coming from my computer screen, I feel God's light and love for me. I also know that the signs I HAVE been asking God to give me have probably been given to me in multiple ways regarding my "next move." I thought I was frozen in looking, but I am happy to report that my inner child took notice and also took some steps to recognize those signs.
I have a follow-up appointment with my OBGYN/surgeon in a couple of weeks to go over the findings from my surgery. I also have a follow-up discussion with my fertility specialist regarding what the next steps are. We have one

perfect embryo left, and after the surgery and what I know so far, my chances of carrying that child myself are probably not the best option for me, my health, and possibly the embryo. That doesn't mean it's over; it just means my path may be taking a turn towards surrogacy, an option I never thought I would entertain, yet here I am. I am taking notice of the signs God has given me as I learn to loosen my grip on my envelope and trust that the plan that lies within is better than anything I could ever imagine. I have to remember, regardless of how often I question it, God's love will always be unwavering and given to me.

Update: The follow-up appointment revealed that a hysterectomy was needed for my overall health and was scheduled and performed in July 2022. After the surgery, we decided that surrogacy wasn't something we wanted to pursue, and we shut the door on having a child of our own for good. As tough as it was, God's plan for me is still being revealed.

Erin Baer

ABOUT THE AUTHOR

Mrs. Erin Baer

Sharing her personal story became the basis for Erin Baer's first book, From Beaten to Badass. The powerfully worded memoir gives readers the strength, hope, and courage to keep going and become the badass they were always meant to be.

Seeing women being silenced for wanting to be strong, courageous, and proud of who they are while moving on from feeling beaten down by life, Erin decided to be a cheerful voice, providing an example whereby circumstances do not define us and that we, too, can be our heroes. Through her writing, coaching, and speaking, Erin encourages women to look within where they will find their power to unleash the badass within.

Erin is the founder of the organization Beaten to Badass, dedicated to empowering those who have been beaten down by life, whether it be by domestic violence, sexual assault, bullying, abandonment, infertility, or however life beats them down. Beaten to badass exists to start the conversation, raise awareness, give back, and implement change.

If you feel defeated or feel life is unfair because of the cards you were dealt, you lose only if you don't learn and don't get back up. You are a Badass! Others' stories inspired Erin to create her first anthology, The Badass Within. Fifteen women share personal, honest, and courageous stories detailing their sadness, joy, and strength. Through sharing their stories, they release the chains of the past and unleash the badass within. They hope that readers will be inspired to discover their badass within and let her shine.

Erin's second anthology, Graceful Growth, was created from the recovery process from several losses in her life and the lives of the six contributing authors. You will discover how each one of these women turned within, found her inner compass, and grew gracefully from losses they thought they might never survive.

Erin holds a BSBA in Business Administration from Rockhurst University and an MBA in Business Management from Avila University. She is now a thriving entrepreneurial badass who lives her passions as a best-selling author, speaker, and coach. Erin has contributed to many book collaborations, including Hold My Crown, Overcoming Heart Blocks, Healing and Growth, and Graced for Prosperity. As with Erin's projects, some proceeds go to empowering women's organizations. She lives in Colorado with her husband, Zach, and their four cats, Taco, Kodak, Leela, and Breckenridge.

GET & STAY CONNECTED @

FB: www.facebook.com/erinbaerbadass

And be Ye Transformed...

Psalm 95:2 - "Let us come into his presence with thanksgiving; let us make a joyful noise to him with songs of praise!"

JACQUELINE LULU BROWN
IN HIS PRESENCE

Totally Transformed

BEYOND THE VEIL OF DIMENSIONS

By: Jacqueline "Pastor LuLu" Brown

The very concept of being in His presence transcends our earthly understanding. To dwell in the presence of God is to tap into realms far beyond the limitations of our physical world, extending into interstellar, higher dimensions that our human eyes cannot perceive. These realms, often spoken of in scriptures, house the throne of God, the angels who worship Him day and night, and the endless expanse of His glory. It is in these higher dimensions where His presence is most tangible, where worship becomes a cosmic symphony, and where the Spirit of God moves freely, unrestricted by time or space.

In today's world, however, many struggle to comprehend this. Our society, increasingly focused on material realities and scientific explanations, often dismisses the unseen as mythical or, at best, metaphorical. This skepticism has seeped into how many view the church, particularly in matters of worship, speaking in tongues, and the indwelling of the Holy Spirit. Some see the expression of the Holy Spirit as a show, a spectacle of man's theatrics, rather than an authentic connection to the divine.

But those who have experienced His presence in the heavenly realms know differently. To stand amid true worship is to enter a different dimension — a place where words fail, and the language of the Spirit takes over.

Speaking in tongues, for example, is not a chaotic babble to the untrained ear; it is the Spirit of God communicating through us in ways our earthly language cannot. It is an interdimensional conversation where the veil between heaven and earth thins, and the heart of God is revealed.

Yet, many need help understanding because they are not operating in these heavenly realms. They are confined to the limitations of earthly logic and understanding. To be in His presence requires a shift in consciousness—a willingness to leave behind what is comfortable and known and enter into the mystery of God. Faith is the portal that grants us access to these dimensions. We encounter God as a concept and a living, breathing reality through faith.

To better understand and experience these divine realms, one can first embrace the practice of *deep meditation and prayer focused on Jesus Christ and the Holy Spirit.* This isn't just any prayer but one of surrender, where you intentionally quiet your mind and allow the Holy Spirit to guide you into more profound revelations. Set aside distractions, enter a stillness space, and actively invite the Lord to reveal Himself. When you open your heart this way, you experience spiritual realities that transcend your everyday perceptions.

Secondly, immerse yourself in *scripture with an emphasis on spiritual discernment.* Many truths about the heavenly realms are hidden within the Word of God and unlocked through the guidance of the Holy Spirit. Study passages that speak of the supernatural encounters of prophets and apostles—such as Ezekiel's visions or Paul's journeys into the third heaven—and seek to understand them not as distant, historical events, but as realities, you can experience in your walk with God today. The Word is alive, and when approached with expectation and faith, it can transport you into those heavenly dimensions.

In these higher dimensions, worship is not bound by the four walls of a church building. The Spirit of God is not contained in religious rituals or traditions. Instead, worship becomes a limitless expression of reverence and adoration, touching the very heart of God. It is a sacred exchange where the finite touches the infinite, and the temporal meets the eternal.

Being in His presence is to step into this otherworldly reality, where miracles are not anomalies but the norm and where the supernatural becomes the natural. Those who worship in Spirit and truth understand that the language of the heavens is far different from that of the earth. They speak in tongues to impress and commune with the divine. They receive the Holy Spirit not as an abstract feeling but as a transformative force that empowers them to live in alignment with God's will.

In His presence, there is fullness of joy. But that joy comes from tapping into realms beyond this world, where the glory of God is not a concept but a living, radiant force. As believers, we are called to ascend, to leave behind the earthly mindsets that limit our understanding, and to enter into the higher dimensions where God dwells. In this place, we truly encounter Him, not just in part, but in His fullness. To those who doubt the authenticity of the church's worship, the speaking in tongues, and the move of the Holy Spirit, I say this: You cannot understand what you have not experienced. You cannot comprehend heavenly dimensions while remaining rooted in earthly limitations. But the invitation to ascend is always open. God is calling us to rise to step into the higher realms of His presence, where our spirits will find the ultimate truth — that He is authentic, that He is near, and that His glory is boundless.

I wish you, the reader, "PEACE, LOVE, LIGHT, JOY, EASE, AND FLOW." JLB

Jacqueline JuJu Brown

ABOUT THE AUTHOR

Jacqueline "Lulu" Brown

Women's Executive Leadership Consultant
ICF Certified Coach
Women's Executive Leadership Trainer
Certified Behavior Practitioner
Transformational Coach & Speaker
Seasoned Retreat Leader | Author
Licensed Reverend | Pastor | Ministerial Counselor
CEO Revolution Ascension LLC

Jacqueline Brown has over 25 years of experience in Ministry, non-profit transitional preparedness, ministerial counseling, and 40+ years in the Information Technology and Engineering corporate arenas.

She is a Serial Entrepreneur, certified behavior practitioner, ICF certified professional coach, best-selling international co-author, transformational speaker, seasoned retreat host and leader, Pastor at "The Most Excellent Way International Ministry, Atlanta Campus, and founder of Revolution Ascension LLC, a coaching and consulting firm dedicated to doing the most profound work with professional, Executive Women at the C-suite level.

What drives Jacqueline *(also endearingly known as Lulu)* is the opportunity to reduce human and organizational suffering, address the need for "Ministering Fresh and Revitalization with Fun," equip people to remove corporate and Ministry burnout, and live with more purpose, grace, and joy.

Jacqueline's consulting and coaching practice focuses on Leadership and women of all colors. She believes that the new era of women's Leadership calls us to step more fully into our role as positive deviants and changemakers. This requires greater attention to self-care, a willingness to reveal what needs to be healed, and the courage to name and pursue our most authentic aspirations. She believes women require this to achieve the freedom, discernment, and integrated life needed to step entirely into their unique purpose on the planet.

Before launching her coaching and consulting practice, Jacqueline spent over 15 of her 40+ career years in global senior leadership roles in high-tech and software-quality engineering. During her travels across the globe, she discovered that women, in their careers, businesses, and Ministries, were feeling the heavy burden of silently carrying their "unsaid" and burnout. These unsaid challenges and burnout statuses are often not openly discussed because of secret shame and the fear of revealing one's true self.

In 2010, Jacqueline's true calling and genius were burning like "fire shut up in her bones." *Additionally, Jacqueline received a deep calling to revolutionize today's women in Ministry and Leadership with a unique message of empowerment and freedom for the masses of Women on a level that is not taught in today's corporate, "religious institutions," or community environments.* Now, as a Transformational Minister and Speaker, ICF (International Coaching Federation) Certified Coach, Elevation Leader, Women's Empowerment Consultant, Mentor, and Licensed Minister, she's spoken, coached, and mentored Women and Young Girls across the world, including India, Africa,

Dubai, the United Kingdom, Australia, Israel, Spain, Antigua, Mexico, and Aruba.

Jacqueline's purpose and focus with her ministry gifting is to provide a safe, sacred space for open, honest, and raw conversation, allowing women in Leadership to explore their challenges to reveal solutions and implementation plans for life. The key outcomes for clients are alignment with Spirit and authenticity, removal of burnout and "fight-flight" syndrome, and unleashing one's Divine Feminine God -given Power that yields results in their lives more extraordinary than ever imagined.

Jacqueline is a phenomenal disrupter, positive deviant, and radical change agent, moving away from the status quo. She teaches "coming out of the box" and not being afraid to "color outside the lines" and is an expert thought leader who helps women go from good to great and from fantastic to phenomenal. She delves into the heart of the matter with solutions to operate authentically and non-conform to the world's systems for success.

Jacqueline provides God ly Faith-Based solutions that free mindsets, remove indoctrination, and release the chains that hold women, particularly women of color, back from ascending to their highest selves. She values innovation, diversity, service, individuality, and equality.

When asked what she wants to be remembered for, she answers, "to lead every woman I encounter to have a bright shining life that sings to their soul." She enjoys making this happen with her phenomenal retreats," AscendHer" Academy, Ministerial Leadership Counseling,

Executive Women's Leadership consulting and training, and keynote speaking engagements.

She is an x4 international best-selling co-author and Co-Chief-in-Editor of Lifestyles and Leisure magazine. Additionally, Jacqueline dramatically enjoys her philanthropic outreach, teaching women in transitional facilities in the USA and faith-based organizations in various parts of Africa. She is a significant supporter of the *"I AM Her International" organization, which assists women in Africa in achieving their life purpose, and she is the CPO (chief program officer) for "THE WAY-OUT MINISTRIES INC.*

Jacqueline is married to retired Captain Kevin Brown and has a blended family with six adult children, 17 grandchildren, and four great-grandchildren.

Revolution Ascension LLC

THE MISSION - FROM THE CEO

"Transformational Healing & Learning for Professional Women" - Revolution Ascension is the catalyst for professional women seeking to amplify their voices and unleash the power of their divine femininity in Leadership. Our mission is clear: to guide women in embracing and executing their authentic selves for unparalleled success. Through tailored consultations with organizations, we empower women leaders to embody authenticity throughout their journey. Our training programs are designed to equip women with the tools to navigate corporate landscapes while staying true to themselves. Revolution Ascension goes beyond mere support and offers transformative experiences that leave clients with actionable insights seamlessly integrated into their daily lives.

THE LULU EXPERIENCE
'Peace, Love, Light, Joy, Ease & Flow' - JLB

GET & STAY CONNECTED @
Website: www.revolutionascension.com
FB: www.facebook.com/revolutionascension
IG: www.instagram.com/revolutionascension
X: https://twitter.com/RevolutionAsce1
https://online.flippingbook.com/view/627772876/
Office: 770-320-7273
Cell: 203-309-8836

LET'S WORK TOGETHER! Engage Jacqueline Brown (Pastor Lulu) to ignite transformative conversations and training that drive lasting change in your organization's leadership landscape.

Please schedule a complimentary call at:
Appointments:
https://calendly.com/revolutionascension/45-minute-consultation
Alignable: https://www.alignable.com/stockbridge-ga/revolution-ascension-llc
LinkedIn: https://www.linkedin.com/in/jacqueline-brown-829723132/

And be Ye Transformed...

John 15:4 - "Abide in me, and I in you. As the branch cannot bear fruit by itself, unless it abides in the vine, neither can you, unless you abide in me."

KENYATTA POWERS-RUCKER

IN HIS PRESENCE

Totally Transformed

A JOURNEY OF FAITH AND CLARITY

By: Mrs. Kenyatta Powers-Rucker

"Trust in the Lord with all your heart and lean not on your understanding; in all your ways submit to Him, and He will make your paths straight."

Proverbs 3:5-6 (NIV)

In this new chapter of my life as a full-time entrepreneur, I navigate the unknowns of building a business—a path filled with excitement and challenges. This transition has made me more aware than ever of the need to be deeply connected to God, to seek His presence continually, and to lean on His guidance. While entrepreneurship brings opportunity, it also brings uncertainty, and the clarity and direction I need can only come from being in the presence of God.

Being in God's presence means much more than seeking Him during distress or when we need answers. It's about cultivating a deep, intimate relationship with Him, where His voice becomes a steady guide amid the noise of life. As I embark on this entrepreneurial journey full-time, I am learning that every decision, every opportunity, and every challenge requires me to be in tune with His will. This path demands more than just my knowledge and abilities—it demands my faith and trust in the One who knows the end from the beginning.

In the stillness of His presence, I find clarity.

Full-time entrepreneurship involves risk, and without God's guidance, it is easy to become lost or overwhelmed. There are moments when I am unsure of the next step when the future seems unclear, and when doubts creep in. But in those moments, I remind myself that God's direction is perfect, and His timing is always right. Being in His presence reminds me that I am not walking this path alone. I have a divine partner invested in my success, not just in business but in living a life that aligns with His purpose for me.

In this season of full-time entrepreneurship, I have realized that more than just achieving business goals, God desires that I live a life of purpose—one that glorifies Him and blesses others. And this, I believe, is the ultimate call for all of us. Whether we are entrepreneurs, leaders, or in any other vocation, God's presence equips us to live purposefully, to make decisions that honor Him, and to impact the world around us. In His presence, we receive the strength to keep going, even when things get tough, and the wisdom to know what steps to take next.

The business world often talks about the importance of clarity—clarity of vision, purpose, and strategy. But as I walk this path as a full-time entrepreneur, I've learned that true clarity comes from aligning with God's will. When we are in His presence, we see things from His perspective. Our vision becomes more precise, our purpose more defined, and our strategy is aligned with His perfect plan. This doesn't mean that challenges won't come; they certainly will. But being in His presence means we can face those challenges with peace that surpasses understanding.

One of the most beautiful aspects of being in God's presence is the strength that comes with it. There is an indescribable power that flows from being connected to the Almighty. When I am in His presence, I feel empowered to run a successful business and be a leader, a mentor, and a light in the marketplace. Full-time entrepreneurship can be mentally and physically draining, but I am constantly renewed in His presence. I draw strength from His word and am reminded of His promises. I find the courage to take bold steps in Him, even when unsure of the outcome.

As I continue this journey, I am more intentional about seeking God's presence daily. I am constantly striving to hear His voice and understand His direction. I know this is a lifelong pursuit that requires dedication and discipline. It is easy to get caught up in the busyness of life and business, but I am learning that true success comes from being still in His presence, listening to His voice, and following His lead.

In this season of full-time entrepreneurship, I also recognize the importance of sharing this journey with others. As a leader, I want to encourage those around me to seek God's presence in their lives. I believe that when we are all aligned with His will, we create a ripple effect of purpose and power in our communities. Being in His presence is not just a personal pursuit; it can transform lives and organizations. When business leaders operate from a place of divine clarity and purpose, we create environments where others can thrive.

Ultimately, being in His presence is about living a life that is pleasing to Him—a life that reflects His love, grace, and power. It's about trusting He knows the way, even when we don't. And it's about finding peace amid uncertainty, knowing that He is with us every step of the way.

As I step into this new chapter as a full-time entrepreneur, I am committed to walking this journey hand in hand with God. As long as I remain in His presence and follow His direction, I will achieve my goals and live a fulfilling, purposeful life aligned with His divine will. This is the ultimate success—knowing that I am living the life God intended for me and that His presence is my constant source of strength and power.

In His presence, I find everything I need to succeed—not just in business, but in life. And I pray that others find the same peace, clarity, and purpose as they seek His presence.

Kenyatta Powers-Rucker

GET & STAY CONNECTED @

Website: www.kenyattapowersrucker.com
IG: @kenyattapowersrucker
LinkedIn - www.linkedin.com/in/kenyatta-powers-rucker-17082b4
FB - www.facebook.com/kenyatta8
TikTok: www.tiktok.com/@kpr814
FB Group - Ladies in Tech
Twitter - https://twitter.com/kenyattaprucker

ABOUT THE AUTHOR

Mrs. Kenyatta Powers-Rucker

Kenyatta Powers-Rucker is an award-winning visionary leader, technology executive, and advocate for diversity and inclusion with over 25 years of experience in state technological governance, agency development, and enterprise project execution. As the former Chief Information Officer (CIO) for the Maryland Department of Human Services, Kenyatta was the first African American female to hold this position. As CIO, she oversaw the department's entire IT infrastructure, managed a $100M annual IT budget, and led over 400 professionals across various technology domains.

Kenyatta serves as Vice President at TriPowers LLC, a minority, woman, and veteran-owned business dedicated to delivering exceptional products and services to government entities. In this role, she continues to lead, focusing on innovation, operational excellence, and empowering government clients through transformative technology solutions.

Beyond her executive roles, Kenyatta is a passionate advocate for underrepresented communities in the tech industry. She founded the Taste of Technology program, which introduces individuals from these communities to the vast opportunities within the tech sector, providing them with the skills and confidence to succeed. Additionally, as the visionary author of the Ladies in Tech Anthology Series, Kenyatta has created a powerful platform for women in technology to share their stories, challenges, and successes, helping to inspire the next generation of female leaders.

Kenyatta is also an international keynote speaker known for her engaging talks encouraging women to step into leadership roles and advocate for greater diversity in the tech industry. Her work has significantly impacted both the national and global stage, influencing corporate policies, inspiring women worldwide, and contributing to a more inclusive technology landscape.

With a solid commitment to mentoring and developing future leaders, Kenyatta ensures that her teams and the communities she serves are prepared to tackle today's challenges and equipped to shape the future of technology. Her leadership, vision, and dedication make her a trailblazer in promoting excellence and diversity within the tech industry.

And be Ye Transformed...

Psalm 42:2 - "My soul thirsts for God, for the living God. When shall I come and appear before God?"

OCTAVIA E. BRADLEY

IN HIS PRESENCE

Totally Transformed

THE POWER OF BEING IN GOD'S PRESENCE

By Mrs. Octavia Bradley

Being in God's presence ignites a fire deep within the soul—a passion that fuels every aspect of our being. It's an impossible fire to extinguish, providing warmth on the coldest days and light on the darkest nights. This fire, combined with empathy, love, and peace, transforms us into reflections of God's image, each day striving to live more like Christ. The Power of Being in God's Presence Over the past year, you might have experienced losses wins, and completed some challenges. You might have lost touch with aligning your life with God's will, but you've gained the ultimate victory—salvation through Jesus Christ. The challenges you faced have brought you here, to this very moment, where God's grace has carried you through. Even when we stray from God's path, His mercy and love are always available, calling us back to the safety of His embrace.

Reflecting on this journey, one scripture comes to mind: For I know the plans I have for you, declares the Lord, plans to prosper you and not to harm you, plans to give you hope and a future." —Jeremiah 29:11 (NIV) It is a reminder that God's plans are always greater than our own. Even when we lose our way or feel our steps have faltered, He is there, guiding us back, refining us through each experience, and showing us what it means to walk in His presence. When we think about being in God's presence, the fruits of the Spirit come to mind: love, joy, peace, patience, kindness, goodness, faithfulness, gentleness, and self-control. These are qualities that God instills in us, traits that reflect His character. Which of these fruits have you mastered thus far? Perhaps love stands out most because to love like Jesus requires more than surface-level affection. It's sacrificial and unconditional, even when it's difficult or painful.

The Word tells us: Above all, love each other deeply because love covers over a multitude of sins." —1 Peter 4:8 (NIV). To love deeply and unconditionally is to embody Christ Himself. It's not a love defined by human conditions or limitations but a love that flows from the heart of God, touching the deepest parts of our souls. To indeed be in God's presence requires sacrifice and surrender. It means letting go of our worldly desires and allowing God to transform us from the inside out. It's letting go of control and trusting God's process, even when it doesn't make sense. God's presence means worshiping, praying, and meditating on His Word. It means setting aside time daily to connect with Him, listen, and align my heart with His.

There's a shift in the atmosphere that brings hope, comfort, and a sense of peace that surpasses all understanding. "Do not be anxious about anything, but in every situation, by prayer and petition, with thanksgiving, present your requests to God. And the peace of God, which transcends all understanding, will guard your hearts and your minds in Christ Jesus." —Philippians 4:6-7 (NIV). A divine exchange happens when we enter into God's presence. Our worries and fears are replaced with His peace. His strength covers our weaknesses. And our doubts are overshadowed by His unwavering truth. Through my trials, I've often asked God, "Why me?" His response, though gentle, was always the same: "Why not you?" At first, it seemed like an answer that didn't quite fit the question, but as I continued to seek Him, I began to understand. Each storm and trial was a test of faith and an opportunity for growth. God molded and shaped me into the person He called me to be. "Consider it pure joy, my brothers and sisters, whenever you face trials of many kinds, because you know that the testing of your faith produces perseverance." —James 1:2-3 (NIV).

These tests weren't meant to harm me but to build a steadfast foundation of faith. To be in God's presence is to trust His process completely. It means showing up for God, even when it's hard, the storms are raging, and even when His way doesn't seem to match our own. As I've walked through various seasons, I've learned that being in God's presence isn't just about feeling His peace or receiving His blessings. It's about surrendering fully to His will and understanding His timing is perfect. It's realizing that my plans will always fall short compared to His grand design for my life.

"Trust in the Lord with all your heart and lean not on your own understanding; in all your ways submit to Him, and He will make your paths straight." —Proverbs 3:5-6 (NIV). To submit is to let go of our preconceived notions, anxieties, and fears. It's to trust that God is leading us, even when the path ahead seems unclear. God's presence is not limited to Sundays or specific times. It's an ongoing relationship, one that requires dedication and intentionality. It's choosing to put Him first in every decision, every thought, and every action. It's choosing to see Him in the small things—like the beauty of nature, the laughter of loved ones, and the quiet moments of solitude.

Think about walking on a soft, plush carpet barefoot. That feeling of comfort, that gentle caress beneath your feet— that's the peace God wants you to feel every time you come into His presence. It's an overwhelming sense of safety, love, and acceptance. So, what have you lost, won, or completed this past year? You might have lost a bit of alignment with God's will, but you've won salvation and the promise of eternal life through Jesus. You've completed the steps God must take to get here—to this place of revelation and understanding.

Today, I encourage you to seek God's presence with a renewed passion. Reflect on His goodness, trust in His process, and embrace the fruits of His Spirit. Because in His presence is fullness of joy, and at His right hand, there are pleasures always (Psalm 16:11).

May your life be forever transformed as you dwell in the beautiful presence of the Most High.

Mrs. Octavia Bradley

GET & STAY CONNECTED @

ABOUT THE AUTHOR

Mrs. Octavia Bradley

Professional Therapist, LSW, Certified Parent Coach

Octavia Bradley is a woman of God, wife, mother, CEO, author, educator, inspirational speaker, Life Enhancement Coach, and Professional Therapist. She obtained her M.A. in Psychology from the University of Phoenix Online and became a Certified Life Coach in 2019. Octavia continues to pursue her studies in Trauma and Mental Health as needed while working to become a Licensed Clinical Therapist. She was born and raised in New York City by her mother and grandmother during her early years. As Langston Hughes wrote, Life for Octavia has not been a crystal stair. Being raised by a gay mother in the late 70's, who was a feared drug lord, was challenging. Her mother was, in her way, an entrepreneur everyone envied until she started using the "crack" product she sold. This led to a life of drugs and jail, which caused Octavia a life cycle of abuse, and she was placed in one of New York's Foster Care Systems, where she learned to survive with her younger sister. Her life was filled with pain and struggle, but out of all she had to do to survive, she has become a phenomenal woman. Because Octavia was a product of the child welfare system in New York, she was most passionate about helping others. She worked to help change people's lives like the wounded families in her childhood.

Octavia worked in the social service field for over 20 years; she was a substance abuse counselor, a case manager for individuals transitioning from prison to home, a case manager for mothers in need, and a family service worker for the foster care system in the state of New Jersey where she currently resides. In August 2015, she received a revelation from God to resign; however, she did not listen and continued until she received another revelation in 2017. She finally resigned from the State of New Jersey and continued her services as an educator and facilitator at several colleges and universities. She has excelled in an online talk show, Let's Talk, where she has won two awards for best talk show and talk show most viewed on Christian Vision Entertainment Network. She is now hosting her podcast Faith 2 Believe to encourage and inspire individuals with inspirational messages. Octavia has written her 1st book, an autobiography titled Leaked Spilling Secrets of Trauma, and her 2nd Book, Reveal 2 Heal Working from the Inside Out.

Now, back to the revelation God has given her to start her Reveal 2 Heal Consulting Services LLC and the Nonprofit Reveal to Heal Consulting Inc. This business has been a product of God's revelation to Octavia. It is geared towards providing resources and mental health services to families and at-risk youth and funding a transitional home for young adults aging out of foster care. Her company comprises individuals with experience and over 50 years of direct social service support, prevention techniques, compassion, and education. Her focus is to put an end to the cycle of generational repetition, such as abuse, poverty, and self-harm. Octavia and her family are here to assist, educate, and refine the mental and emotional state of individuals affected by trauma or painful experiences. Because we are in a world that is forever changing, our goal is to go into the homes and have courageous conversations with families who are struggling from day-to-day life stressors and teach them healthy and positive ways to live and talk about feelings and emotions so silence and death caused by these day-to-day life stressors could be alleviated. We want to bring communication, understanding, kindness, patience, and love into our families' homes. God revealed to Octavia how to complete this goal by providing therapy and education to young children and bringing families together.

Octavia has finally started constructing TEACH—a therapeutic & Education Academy for children. The mission is to provide high-quality early childcare, therapy, and education to diverse children and develop their academic, social, and emotional learning through close and thoughtful partnerships with educators, families, child development professionals, and local community and state agencies. It's time to take back our community and allow the village of support and resources into your homes.

And be Ye Transformed...

Hebrews 10:22 - "Let us draw near with a true heart in full assurance of faith, with our hearts sprinkled clean from an evil conscience and our bodies washed with pure water."

ELDER AILEEN HILL, DTM

IN HIS PRESENCE

Favour is deceitful, and beauty is vain: But a woman that feareth the LORD, she shall be praised.
Proverbs 31:30

Totally Transformed

WALKING WITH THE FATHER

By: Elder Aileen Hill, DTM

I have no greater joy than hearing my children walk in the truth. - 3 John 4, NIV

Living in Philadelphia, PA, in March of 2020, COVID-19 affected everyone, including myself. My employers furloughed me, my church conducted brief Sunday services with few members in attendance, my Toastmasters club met online via ZOOM, and my "go-to place to work out" at the YMCA was closed. Watching the news and listening to the talk radio, there was no optimism in sight as to when there will be a clear path from this pandemic.

People were becoming sick, dying from this deadly disease, or fearing to go outside and preferred home deliveries. As these events were unfolding, I refused to accept this status quo. Suddenly, inspiration arose inside of me to do something by encouraging my Facebook family and friends to move. June 2020 began the walking challenges towards 10,000 steps; those who felt physically limited were challenged to at least walk around the block, move their extremities, walk up & down the steps, or choose their favorite activity to keep MOVING. I've posted videos and pictures of my walks on Facebook and started seeing positive reactions. My mask covers my nose and mouth while utilizing the sidewalks of Philadelphia; I've continued this journey during the pandemic.

One day, as I concluded one of my walks, I went to my car sitting on the driver's side, reflecting on the responses of those who felt inspired and encouraged. I asked God, "What should I name this walking journey that you have me doing?" That's when I heard the Lord say: Walking With The Father. All I can say is, "Wow," especially the times we live in. I believe we all need to have that closer walk with God, be in good health, and prosper in every aspect of our lives (3 John 1:2). My walk begins with a salutation and declaration from Psalm 118:24: "This is the day which the Lord hath made; we will (I will, you will) rejoice and be glad in it." My walks and step counts are recorded while encouraging social media users to keep moving and not let this pandemic get the best of us.

I made adjustments to my walking regimen as the weather began to change, not knowing another change would take place in my relocation to Sumter, South Carolina, upon my mother's diagnosis of Dementia & Alzheimer's Disease. My new chapter of living in SC was hampered by not having my consistent walks with Father God. One of my girlfriends from Philadelphia called to check in on me and inspired me with these words: "Continue with your Walking With The Father," which gave me the boost to locate walking parks or trails to continue this journey.

I truly needed the Lord's guidance upon a Televisit conversation with my Doctor in Philly concerning increased blood levels trending towards Pre-Diabetic. Transferring my medical files to Tandem Health in Sumter, SC, I arranged to see a Physician. To hear a Diabetic Diagnosis in Dec. 2021 from the Residency Doctor and disparaging remarks from the Attending Doctor constantly saying: "You have Diabetes," Walking With The Father became a whole new initiative toward healthy eating and lifestyle. Changes were made by walking, changing my eating habits, taking medications with a resolve to become medicine-free, increasing my exercise routine at the Sumter YMCA, and applying the word of God. My A1C at the start was 9.4 with a weight of 220 lb.; when writing this chapter in 2023, my weight was 195 lbs. with an A1C of 6.5. My weight and A1C fluctuate occasionally; however, I am trending downward in the right direction, in which I praise God.

Walking With The Father has become the name of my ministry to bring a holistic approach to the general public, inside & out, through healthy lifestyle, healthy weight & identifying the lack of nutritious food choices in their community. I sought the Lord's guidance in starting this nonprofit with assistance from a business strategist. While waiting for the South Carolina Business Entities' confirmation on receiving the Articles of Incorporation and the 501 (c)(3) attachment, I recalled some profound nuggets from an instructor upon attending a Monday evening Cardio workout at the Sumter YMCA.

She dropped some awesome nuggets about how she loves to walk and that her Father God keeps her healthy by continuing to walk. I began to reflect on my journey of walking since the beginning of the COVID-19 pandemic in March 2020 and encourage others to do the same. On February 6, 2024, Walking With The Father Ministries became a non-profit ministry. I will obtain a personal fitness training certification and education from the experts to become a qualified fitness instructor.

Elder Aileen J. Hill

GET & STAY CONNECTED @

Email: walkingwiththefather100@gmail.com
FB: www.facebook.com/aileen.hill.5/
IG: www.instagram.com/aileen.hill.5/
LinkedIn: www.linkedin.com/in/aileen-hill-68712b87/

ABOUT THE AUTHOR

Elder Aileen J. Hill

Aileen Joyce Hill is a licensed evangelist and serves on the Board of Elders at Divine Destiny Community Fellowship, where her Pastors are Dwaine and Minette Ross. A native of the Bronx, NY, educated in the NYC public school system, she received her bachelor's degree at Syracuse University in Fine Arts and a master's degree at Drexel University in Arts Administration & Arcadia University in Elementary Education. Her career path has made her marketable to specialize in the Administrative, Non-Profit, and Education Sectors.

Aileen is the #1 Amazon Best Seller Author in: "OWN It!" Anthology: It's Your Life "OWN It!" Unapologetically and 365 Days to "OWN It!" Transformation - Anthology Journal. Her chapter, "Rooted and Grounded," was inspired by her Pastor during a great job opportunity that became a loss in a short time. Her Pastor's inspiration gave her the grit not to "stay in the dumps" but to "an assignment more significant than this.

She has written two chapters for two anthology projects, "Walking With The Father" for 'In His Presence' Anthology and "A Meeting With Myself" for 'Unleashed Anthology. Her ministry, Walking With The Father Ministries, brings a holistic approach to the general public, inside & out, through healthy lifestyle, healthy weight & identifying the lack of nutritious food choices in their community. Her ministry will also further other core aspects of daily living.

And be Ye Transformed...

Acts 17:27 - "That they should seek God, and perhaps feel their way toward him and find him. Yet he is actually not far from each one of us."

DITHRA SANDS

IN HIS PRESENCE

Totally Transformed

MY GOD IS AN AWESOME GOD

By: Dithra Sands

My God is incredible; my life, business, and career would not be the same without him. I can feel his spirit within me when I am in his presence. It is like a ray of sunshine that cannot wait to shine. I only want to worship him until I can't anymore; that is a fantastic feeling. Things did not always go the way that I planned, but once I put God first in my life and my belief in his word. Matthew 6:33 says, "But seek ye first the kingdom of God, and his righteousness; and all these things shall be added unto you." Things became very different in my life. His word is his promise to us; he is a man who does not lie.

By being in his presence and listening to him speak to you, he guides you in the direction you should be going. What he has done for me in my life is unexplainable. He has given me strategies that connect me with people physically and spiritually, and we are on the same mission to win souls and help individuals move to the next level in their lives. Chills run down my arms when I think of what he has done for me. My God is an awesome God who will supply your every need. There is a glow in me that others see. You walk with your head up and confidently because you always have that perfect companion with you. Now, it has not always been this way for me. Initially, I struggled in my life, business, and career. When I decided that I wanted to change the direction I was going in. I had to change my mindset and what was in my heart. I had to become one with the Lord by being a servant. When you can serve and appreciate the little things in life, things start changing. Your flesh begins to die so that more of the Lord can enter your life. Sometimes, you must be still and let the Lord guide you to your destiny. Individuals can feel your spirit when they interact with you. Sometimes, you will just get blessings out of the blue. Individuals will show you favor without you asking. You will have doors closed on you, which will be lessons you will learn. You will have doors open to you as well. There are people out there waiting on what we have to offer, whether it be a product, service, inspirational words of encouragement, or educational guidance.

When you start a business and put God first, he will show you the unthinkable. He will give you what is needed to succeed in life. Make sure you put God first, no matter what you are directed to do. At that point, things start happening for you. Time after time, we want to rush God for what we want in life, Business, and Career. But the Lord will not give you anything until he sees that you are ready and in a place to receive what he has for you. What do you want most in your life, business, and career? You can have those very things. Stay focused on the Lord, and remove all distractions that prevent you from getting closer to him. Continue to live your life according to Jesus, and he will see that you live a life of abundance in all areas. I am grateful and thankful for him accepting me as his child. Philippians 4:13 – "I can do all things through Christ which strengthened me."

Dithra Sands

ABOUT THE AUTHOR

Mrs. Dithra Sands

Dithra (Deetra) Sands was born in Neptune, NJ. An Independent Certified Financial Representative with Primerica for more than 20+ years who enjoys helping all in need with their finances. She travels throughout New Jersey sharing her expertise on "How Money Works" through Financial Literacy Workshops that are entirely free to Organizations, Communities, Schools, and Corporations. Dee has been featured on Blog Talk Radio – Take Center Stage and Own it, Real Talk W/Dr. Rollins-Fells, and a monthly spot-on De La Mano Con Lucy. She was also featured in *Take Center Stage. Own it Magazine, Bella*, the Influencer Issue, and the 50 0n Fire Project (50 women of color, Living, Loving, Learning, and lit at 50.

One of her passions is to educate women on how to take control of their financial future. She mentors individuals who want a career in Financial Services by showing them how to get licensed while being trained and developed as they build their own Financial Services businesses This also gives individuals the opportunity to manage their finances. Dee will continue to share her expertise with everyone. She interacts with many families that need more education regarding Life Insurance. Dee is on a crusade to educate as many families as possible to get and have adequate Life Insurance.

Dee is currently a member of the Entrepreneurial Think Tank for Women North Jersey (ETT Women) Organizational group, a community of women entrepreneurs who network with intention. They learn from and support each other in personal and business development. She is a member of Promote-Her, a National Network for Women, and she leads business, community, and religious organizations. Also, a Network of Sisterly Support, whereas "When You Win, I Win, Sis" is our motto.

Dee has taken time out and volunteered her services with several organizations, such as the Relay for Life Newark, NJ, and The African American Heritage Parade Organization (AAHPO), to give back to the community. Dee believes knowledge is power only if used to help someone else.

Dithra (Deetra) Sands is a highly rated Life Insurance Representative with 20+ years of experience as an Agent and Financial Coach. Dee's passion is to educate individuals, groups, and organizations on how to take control of their financial future. She mentors people on how to have a career in financial services. The first thing to have established in your financial game plan is income protection (Life Insurance). She partners with Churches, Schools, and Women's Organizations for Leadership classes and financial workshops.

Get & Stay Connected @

Cell Phone: 732-754-8793
Email: Dsands@primerica.com
Website: Deesands.com
            www.primerica.com/Deesands

LinkedIn: http://linkedin.com/in/deesands
Facebook: https://www.facebook.com/Dee.Sandz
IG: https://www.instagram.com/iamdee_sands

And be Ye Transformed...

Psalm 84:10 - "For a day in your courts is better than a thousand elsewhere. I would rather be a doorkeeper in the house of my God than dwell in the tents of wickedness."

REV. DR. JOWANDA ROLLIN-FELLS

IN HIS PRESENCE

Totally Transformed

THE PRESENCE OF GOD IS NECESSARY

By: Rev. Dr. JoWanda Rollin-Fells

Sometimes, life can be overwhelming and cause us to feel like we are being crushed under the weight of it all. In these moments, we often try to figure out a quick solution to relieve the pressure or an exit strategy to release us from the anguish of it all. In these moments, I want to encourage you with a familiar scripture found in the bible.

> *Matthew 6:22 – Seek the kingdom of God and His righteousness first, and all these things will also be given to you.*

We try to get in his presence when we seek God and his righteousness. Psalms 16:11 tells us that God will show us the paths of life and that there is fullness of joy in his presence.

Why do we need the presence of God in our lives?

The answer is simple because the presence of God is necessary to know how to flow, grow, and walk in authority.

The presence of God is necessary to flow.

There are moments when life makes sense, and everything is stable and predictable. In these smooth moments, everything goes according to plan. The stability of things brings comfort and often a sense of peace.

Then, there are those whirlwind moments that appear and are instantaneously volatile. These are the times when life can be demanding and challenging. You may have to make tough decisions but are unclear about what to do. Time may be of the essence, and there is the pressure that the clock is ticking and everything is needed NOW. Stress and anxiety may pile upon and before you know it, you are screaming at the top of your lungs.

I encourage you to pause and get into the presence of God. Pray and ask Him for guidance, wisdom, and courage to do what He has instructed. Whether the moment is particular or uncertain, know that God is there. If you lean into His presence, He can guide you through the delicate balance of knowing what to do, when, and how to do it. God's presence is necessary to understand how to flow.

The presence of God is necessary to grow.

There are moments in life when you observe the physical seasons change. You sense the cooling of the temperatures and watch the fullness of the trees transition to colorful leaves and bare branches. Beyond observing nature, there may be moments when you notice a difference in people and the spirit of things. Things in life are subject to change, and the accompanying transition period is inescapable.

When I built my home, there was a little sapling in the backyard. My father decided not to pull it up as he cared for the lawn. He thought it would make a good shade tree someday. We affectionately called the sapling "The Jordyn Tree" after my daughter who was three at the time. It has been 18 years, and we have watched my daughter, and this tree grow and change. Recently, my daughter came home from college and commented on how the tree is now as tall as the house. We reminisced about how it started as a thin, weed-looking plant and how long the process has been for it to grow. She commented how, at times, she felt like her namesake tree had to stay rooted and grounded even though the seasons had changed all around her. I encouraged her that when life feels uncertain, she leans into the presence of God.

The Bible states that God is the same yesterday, today, and forever. In God, you can find consistency not available anywhere else in creation. His presence matures you and guides you through transitions. Like the Jordyn Tree, God's presence is necessary for you to grow.

The presence of God is necessary to walk in authority.

The highs and lows of life ebb and flow like the tide. Oceans of blessings and goodwill can abound and overtake you in one moment and then seemingly pull back just out of reach at other times. This up and down can often affect your confidence. Fear can creep in, and it is usually accompanied by worry and doubt. Before you know it, negative self-talk speaks up, and the mind game begins.

I want to encourage you to know that regardless of what you see or feel in your flesh, there is a place of solace for your spirit and soul. The Word of God reassures us that He is our comforter, refuge, and fortress. The Word of God says that He can cover us. The Word of God assures us that we don't have to be afraid. His presence is necessary so we can walk confidently and not in fear. Being in God's presence allows us to walk with and in authority. Don't worry about the winds and the waves. Trust God and walk on water.

I am so thankful we have a God who loves us the way He does! I encourage you to strive daily to get into the presence of God. It is necessary to flow, grow, and walk with authority.

Rev. Dr. JolJanda Rollins-Fells

GET & STAY CONNECTED @

Website: spiritofexcellencellc.com
Email: spiritofexcellence.co@gmail.com
Social Media:
#REALTalkw/DrRollinsFells
#Po1.Ministry
www.drrealtalk.com

ABOUT THE AUTHOR

Rev. Dr. JoWanda Rollins-Fells

INSPIRATIONAL SPEAKER, COACH, TRAINER, MINISTER.
"We Don't Compete; We Create!"
Minister, Consultant, and CEO

Mission - To empower and inspire lives

Dr. JoWanda Rollins-Fells is the CEO of Spirit of Excellence LLC, where she provides coaching and a full suite of marketing platforms to authors, speakers, coaches, and ministers to increase their reach and visibility. She owns Spirit of Excellence TV, Power of One Ministry TV, Power of One Magazine, and Power of One Radio.

Dr. Rollins-Fells ministers to the masses through her signature REAL Talk framework of Reframing Reality, Empowering Vision, Activating Faith, and Liberating Legacy. She is a best-selling author and curator of the #MadeforThis clothing line. She is a proud graduate of Hampton University and Capella University. Her doctorate has provided her with an understanding of people, processes, motivation, and transformation.

Dr. Rollins-Fells is a wife, mother, and minister. She thanks God for giving her the wisdom and strength for the legacy she is living and the legacy she is building to extend for generations.

And be Ye Transformed...

Psalm 100:2 - "Serve the Lord with gladness! Come into his presence with singing!"

CONSTANCE PHILLIPS

IN HIS PRESENCE

Totally Transformed

ISOLATION LEADS TO ELEVATION

Ms. Constance Phillips

Sitting in the mental hospital, I see now that's what God does to test your patience and faith. I spazzed out; my mind was slipping worse than a bad transmission. This mental process is profound. However, I know I will go in like a sheep and come out roaring like a lion. Isolation is when I hear God. He speaks so loud and clear. I understand that God is doing something new this season, and I must be patient with the process.

For the past three years, I have been dealing with mental illness. I have been in the behavioral health hospital twice. Each time, I felt restored after completing a 4-day stint. My family has dealt with mental illness for years; however, the majority haven't been professionally diagnosed. The hardest part about dealing with mental illness is that it is hidden from the naked eye. You can see a physical disability and can quickly identify it. Mental illness, unfortunately, isn't the same.

The best way I can explain it is that there are excellent days, but then there are weeks, sometimes months when depression rides my back. It's like a light switch of sadness that kicks in, and I must ride the wave. I will lean more into God when I have those waves of sorrow. I also realize and expect to have good days and bad days. When the evil days come, I am thankful and appreciative of all the good days that I've had. The good ones outweigh the bad ones.

I have spent the last three years ensuring that I stay medicated. That is the hardest part of the diagnosis for me because I don't like to take pills. I rarely want to take preventative medication. I have sought psychiatric help to ensure my mind doesn't derail; however, there is only so much I can do. I find myself giving myself grace. I have been through a lot since my medical diagnosis, and I understand that I have a long road ahead of me. I refuse to quit. I realize that I hear my voice more than anyone else's. I make it a point to talk to myself nicely and say things that make me feel good.

My most excellent refuge is listening to music, driving, or writing. My soul is a lover of all music. Writing these days comes in all forms, either typing or handwriting. It is soothing for me to get my thoughts outside of my brain. Being in God's presence for me brings me peace. God spoke loudly when I was working, especially when driving for Amazon. It was during that time when I would usher God in with praises. I found that God loves to be praised and worshiped. I would just ride and pray for hours. It was peaceful to ride through different neighborhoods and dream of the possibility of providing my children with a much larger home, land, pool, and animals on our land.

My backyard is a nice size. For most of the summer, I sat outside in the mornings and enjoyed my tea. I would watch the birds and the different animals that would come into my backyard. It was during that time that I became appreciative of nature. God works uniquely and will be honored in every way he deems suitable. We have to permit God to work on us. There will be hard times when we get on the potter's wheel to be molded, but that's God's way of smoothing out the kinks. I will forever be on the Potter's wheel because we constantly evolve into who and what God wants us to be.

Constance Phillips

GET & STAY CONNECTED @
FB: @ConstanceGray

ABOUT THE AUTHOR

Ms. Constance Phillips

Serial Entrepreneur

Constance Phillips-Gray was born and raised in Saint Louis, Missouri, where she continues to live.

Constance is an enterprising individual, a life insurance agent, and a Mary Kay representative. She operates a family-run cleaning and logistics company. Her children are her most significant source of pride and joy; without them, she feels incomplete.

As an author, Constance has become a 4x Amazon bestseller and has contributed as a co-author to six anthologies.

She has earned an associate's degree and a certificate in Business Management from Columbia College.

Beyond her professional endeavors and caring for her children, Constance harbors a passion for reading, writing, and embracing her newfound faith journey with Jesus. Committed to volunteering and philanthropy, she regularly donates blood and selflessly offers her time to non-profit organizations.

And be Ye Transformed...

Psalm 145:18 - "The Lord is near to all who call on him, to all who call on him in truth."

COURTNEY CLARK

IN HIS PRESENCE

Totally Transformed

FINDING PEACE IN GOD'S PRESENCE

Courtney Clark

I feel grounded, whole, and complete in His presence. There's a profound stillness when I'm with Him. It's as if the world stands still, and I am calm. To be in God's presence is to be at peace because He embodies peace. We often talk about having peace of mind, but God is that peace for me.

In those quiet moments, I can hear Him profoundly and loudly. It's a paradox that in the silence, His voice becomes the most prominent sound. We often find ourselves surrounded by chaos and turmoil from the world around us, feeling trapped with no way out. We focus on the circumstances instead of looking inward, where our genuine connection with God lies.

When I encounter God, all chaos fades away because He is there in the midst of it all. He only needed me to draw near Him. He has never left me, and He never will. It is I who sometimes choose to distance myself from Him.

During difficult times, we often ask God to change our situations, not realizing that He places us in these situations to change us. When we face trials and tribulations, we grow stronger and more resilient. In these moments of adversity, we can experience God's presence most profoundly.

In God's presence, I find an unshakable sense of grounding. No matter what storms rage around me, I remain steadfast because I know He is with me. This grounding is not just a fleeting feeling; it's a deep-seated assurance that I am never alone.

This sense of wholeness and completeness in His presence reminds me that I am enough just as I am. I don't need to strive for perfection or approval from others. In God's eyes, I am already complete. This realization brings immense peace and contentment.

I can face the world with renewed strength and clarity when calm in God's presence. The noise and distractions of the world lose their power over me. I can focus on what truly matters and make decisions with a clear mind and a peaceful heart.

To be in God's presence is to experience a peace that surpasses all understanding. It is a peace that the world cannot give or take away. It is a constant peace, even amid life's most challenging moments.

We often seek peace of mind through external means, but true peace comes from within. It comes from our connection with God. When we cultivate this inner peace, we can navigate life's ups and downs with grace and resilience.

In conclusion, being in God's presence brings me a sense of grounding, wholeness, and calmness. It allows me to rise above the chaos and turmoil of the world and find peace in His presence. This peace depends not on external circumstances but on my connection with God. When I draw near Him, I see He has always been there, waiting for me to return. Through trials and tribulations, I am reminded that God uses these experiences to shape and strengthen me. In His presence, I find the peace that surpasses all understanding, and I am genuinely grateful.

Courtney Clark

ABOUT THE AUTHOR

Courtney Clark

Certified Life Coach- 12:11 Empowerment Life Coaching, LLC

Courtney Clark is a dedicated life coach specializing in spirituality, self-love, and personal growth, focusing on empowering individuals. Courtney supports clients in overcoming challenges, setting goals, and achieving their dreams. Through personalized coaching,

Courtney helps offenders transition from prison, mentors' teens, and assists in business start-ups, all while fostering confidence and unapologetic living. With a unique blend of compassion and expertise, Courtney is committed to guiding others to a fulfilling and purposeful life.

FB: SimplyCourt – Vibe Higher
TikTok: @simplycourt_vibehigher?
IG: @simplycourt_vibehigher24/
Publication:
www.flawedandstillfavoredcourtneyoliver.now.site/home

Publication: www.lulu.com/shop/courtney-oliver/the-audacity-to-be-empowered/paperback/product-grnv9k.html

Publication: www.amazon.com/dp/B0D7HRWWDC
Website: www.simple-courtney-vibe-higher.netlify.app

And be Ye Transformed...

Colossians 3:1-2 - "If then you have been raised with Christ, seek the things that are above, where Christ is, seated at the right hand of God. Set your minds on things that are above, not on things that are on earth."

PENNIE STALLWORTH

IN HIS PRESENCE

Totally Transformed

FINDING REST AND JOY IN GOD'S PRESENCE:
The Power of Being Fully Present with Him

Pennie Stallworth

A daily ritual in the world is to take attendance. Some are called out by name with a response of present or here. However, the method the goal is to be acknowledged as in your assigned place. Lord, I am here. This is how I withstand the relentless pursuit of the enemy. Being in His presence is more than merely being physically somewhere—it encompasses a maximum engagement of mind, spirit, and demeanor. An invitation requesting your presence asks for more than your body to show up; it's asking for your whole being. This concept of presence takes on a profound meaning in a spiritual context, particularly considering that God's invitation extends to us through Christ Jesus.

He invites us to come into His presence and abide with Him eternally. Accepting this invitation means stepping into a space where I find my most profound joy, peace, and solace. In our fast-paced, modern world, we often hear, "Where are you?". The inquiry isn't just about physical location, whether from family, friends, or supervisors. It's also a subtle request for mental and emotional presence to ensure we are connected and engaged. This need for reassurance and connection reflects a broader human desire for presence—not just from those around us but from someone incredible.

God's presence is the connection between creator and creation.

His presence never moves. I may get distracted, finding myself out of His sacred presence of refuge, protection, and abundant blessings. God's invitation to join Him in this space is constant and unwavering. It's a call to come as I am, with all my burdens and worries, and find rest in His embrace.

There was a time when, during my struggles, I would question God's presence. "God, where are You?" This report shows that I am failing where my performance has always been exceptional. I did not immediately recognize that I relied on my limited strength, knowledge, and experience. Then, as I grew in my understanding of God's sovereignty, I began to see things differently. I realized that every challenge was not an obstruction but an opportunity to lean into His wisdom and trust in His plan.

Resting in God doesn't mean passivity. It's not about sitting back and doing nothing. For me, it often means actively seeking His presence through prayer, reading the Bible, and simply being still before Him. In these moments of quiet reflection, I find the answers, comfort, and direction I need to move forward in ways that honor Him. It's a dynamic relationship where I am both listening and responding, resting and acting. I've learned to turn to worship when faced with the enemy's tactics—whether through fear, doubt, or discouragement. Instead of succumbing to despair, I recount all God has done for me. I remind myself of His past faithfulness and call on the ministering angels He has provided for my comfort and protection. In worship, I find the strength to accept correction and grow, knowing that each lesson is part of my spiritual journey. Even in dangerous situations, I've found that I can rest in God's presence. Psalm 91 has become my shield, a reminder of His protection, while Psalm 23 comforts me with the assurance that I lack nothing when He is with me. These scriptures reinforce that God is always with me, guiding, protecting, and blessing me, no matter the circumstances.

In God's presence, I find joy that is not dependent on external circumstances but rooted in the profound assurance that I am never alone. I can rest in this sacred space, knowing He is in control. This joy is the fulfillment of God's promise, as expressed in John 15:11: "I have told you these things so that My joy and delight may be in you, and that your joy may be made complete and overflowing." This verse reminds us that God's joy is not just for Him but also for us. It is a joy meant to fill us, overflow, and guide us into a light that fulfills our needs and glorifies God.

In conclusion, the presence of God is where I find my true joy and peace. It is a place of refuge and strength where I can rest and be renewed. God's invitation to enter this sacred space is always open, a constant reminder that I can always find my way back to Him, no matter where I am physically or emotionally. I am whole, complete, and overflowing with joy in His presence.

Pennie Stallworth

ABOUT THE AUTHOR

Pennie Stallworth.

D.Min, MSEd, BSEd, CEAP

Pennie Stallworth is a Certified Employee Assistance Professional specializing in Training. She holds an MSEd in Social and Emotional Maladjustment, a degree in Elementary and Special Education, and a D.Min in Religious Education. She excels in developing training curricula on Conflict Resolution, Stress and Anger Management, and Self-Esteem. Her extensive international and domestic experience enriches her ability to guide others in time management, goal setting, and personal growth.

The Vision: Empowering individuals with 'Information for Life' to foster self-awareness, self-worth, and personal effectiveness, enabling them to realize their true potential

The mission is to deliver 'Information for Life' that fosters self-awareness, self-worth, and respect, empowering individuals to understand their development and enhance personal effectiveness.

FB: www.facebook.com/pennie.stallworth
IG: www.instagram.com/penniestallworth
LinkedIn: www.linkedin.com/in/pennie-stallworth-97bb8070

And be Ye Transformed...

Matthew 5:8 - "Blessed are the pure in heart, for they shall see God."

JOANNE WALKER
IN HIS PRESENCE

Totally Transformed

THE GREATNESS OF GOD'S PRESENCE

Joanne Walker

"As the deer longs for streams of water, so I long for you, O God." —Psalm 42:1

I have been a born-again believer of Jesus Christ for 50 years and a Licensed and Ordained Minister and servant of the LORD for 34 years.

I have yet to understand "the greatness of God's presence." However, through the years, God in love, mercy, and grace has allowed me to experience only a portion of His presence.

In 2000, I experienced a drought! The well in my physical life was dry. It left me in the line of unemployment, penniless, and no transportation. It was as if I was in a place where the sun was hidden behind a dark cloud and would never shine again. I was a prisoner without hope, locked within the walls of external life's circumstances. Yet, God's love and mercy permitted me to have a place to call home with my mother, sister, and brother-in-law.

However, this was not the worst of my dilemma. Not only was I experiencing an external drought, but I was also experiencing a spiritual drought in a rush to please God. Attend every church service and Bible Study, saying "yes" to every preaching engagement, counseling numerous individuals, both the saved and unsaved. However, in the attempt to do all, I thought God wanted of me. I had neglected a significant person, "me." I was so busy trying to be everything to everyone else I had forgotten "me." I had spent my days feeding everyone else and, in the process, had unintentionally ignored 'my spirit.' I was reminded of Psalm 42:1, "As the deer longed for streams of water, so I long for you, O, God."

How many of you have been, or are placed in your life, that you desire a fresh soaking of the presence of the Holy Spirit in the depth of your spirit? "I did!" And I found a desire for His presence more than anything or anyone. I knew there was only one way to Him. My mother, the late Tamer Williams, taught me the importance of seeking God. I still hear her voice today; "Joanne, take yourself to a task and pray. This was her way of telling my sibling and me that prayer is the only way to get into the presence of God. And so, it was at this time I sought the Lord through prayer and reading His word. I sought to find the "secret place."

But here is where my prayer journey became more amazing than I ever dreamed. It happened one night while I was on my knees praying, God revealed a vision: "In the vision, I saw myself in a cave. I was seated on the cave floor, looking toward its only exit. However, I noted that my outlet was blocked by what looked like a large stone, which served as a shut door. There was no way out and no way to escape. But this wasn't the most fantastic part. The unique part was that I was not alone. Someone else was in the cave with me. I knew this because I felt His arm around me.

As I turned my body to look at Him, I heard the voice of my LORD speaking directly to me: 'Joanne, I have permitted those things in which you suffer to slow you down so that you may give attention to my voice. You had become so busy with the things you thought were pleasing in my eyes that you neglected to seek to know ME. You were so busy ministering to others that you failed to allow my Spirit to minister to you. It must be replenished and renewed with a fresh anointing for the next ministry level. I am the ONLY One who can and will remove the stone that blocks your way out. It is a process that you must go through. The timing of its removal is in MY HAND!'"

It was at this time that I could feel the shifting of fear and anxiety to a place of peace and serenity. It was also then that I knew I was in the womb of His Holy Spirit. I know that expression may sound crazy to some people. But it was in that place, the cave, that God fed and watered me with and in his Spirit. In the "cave of God's Womb, He grew, watering and nourishing me with the "Fruit of His Spirit." Needless to say, "God removed the stone, and I walked out of the cave of His womb." It took three years, but in 2003, I came out empowered by the Holy Spirit and moved into the next level of Ministry.

My friends, as most of you may know, the process is never easy. It comes with many challenges. There are three things I have noted in every process that I have encountered: "humbling myself before the Lord, surrendering my will and accepting His Will, Seeking His forgiveness, Remembering His God's love for me, and last of all, praising God for the process. For it is in the process that the rain does come; we are cared for, watered, and gain strength. I know whether I am seated in the cave of His womb or at a dinner table gazing into his eyes! I am still in the Greatness of His Presence. The Greatness of God's Is He Is with Us at All Times.

The keys to this are to remember:

1. The key to being in the greatness of God's Presence may not be what you expect.
2. The key to getting into His presence is being humble, seek forgiveness, be prayerful, & Praise Him.
3. The key is giving attention to the indwelling Holy Spirit.
4. The process may not be easy, but it is worth it.
5. God will never leave or abandon you.
6. Draw closer to God and enter into His Presence.

CAN YOU THINK OF A TIME IN YOUR LIFE YOU MIGHT HAVE ENTERED THE PRESENCE OF GOD AND DID NOT REALIZE IT?

Joanne Walker

ABOUT THE AUTHOR

Joanne Walker

Prophetess Joanne Walker (Founder & CEO) God Got It Ministry God Got It Ministry was created and designed by the hands of God. Our vision is to reach out to individuals through the proclamation of the Gospel of Jesus Christ, testimonies, helping, and giving through the expression of God's love.

Prophetess Joanne Walker is a Licensed and Ordained Minister of the gospel of Jesus Christ. She lives in Virginia. She is a preacher, teacher, Intercessor & prayer warrior, and spiritual counselor to many individuals. Prophetess Walke is the Founder and CEO of God Got It Ministry.

She and the GGIM team outreach ministry are instrumental in helping to address the needs of many individuals in the community and other states. (providing food, clothing, monetary love & gifts offerings). Most of all, Prophetess Walker's greatest desire and prayer is that all will come to know Jesus as Lord and Savior.

GET & STAY CONNECTED:
FB: www.facebook.com/God GotItministry/
Email: jw2038592@gmail.com

And be Ye Transformed...

Philippians 4:5 - "Let your reasonableness be known to everyone. The Lord is at hand."

SAUNDRA YVONNE WERTS

IN HIS PRESENCE

Totally Transformed

THE PRESENCE OF GOD

Saundra Yvonne Werts

The word presence in Hebrew is "panim," which means face.

As a believer, I realized that the Presence of God, or getting before God's Face, would help me become God-inside-minded. I began to see and know that Christ abiding in me was the Hope of Glory. Entering the Presence of God has allowed the Holy Spirit to lead and guide me to all truth.

Men and women who have made a quality decision to press into the presence of God reap many benefits. The scriptures state, "In God's presence is fullness of joy, and at his right hand are pleasures forever.

You may be wondering how to get into the Presence of God. One of the things you must recognize about the Presence of God is that it isn't just a place you come to visit as you go to church or visit someone at their home. It is the place where you live; it's a dwelling place. The Presence of God moves with you wherever you go. Listen to what God told Moses in Ex. 33:14: "My presence shall go with you, and I will give you rest."

I enter God's presence through Thanksgiving and Praise. Thanksgiving honors God for what He has done, and praise honors God for who He is. When you offer thanksgiving and praise, you are making a joyful noise. Getting into His Word is another way to enter His Presence. As I began to read and study the Word of God, my mind was renewed, and I was transformed and started to become conformed to the image of Christ.

Getting into the Word of God changed my thought patterns, habits, desires, attitudes, and perspective. Romans 12:1,2. Make a quality decision to get into His Word and study it, as 2 Timothy 2:15 states, so that you can correctly handle the Word of God.

Another way to cultivate God's presence is through prayer. I'm not talking about "Now I lay me down to sleep; I pray the Lord my soul to keep" prayers. I'm talking about moving into a realm where you and God speak to each other as intimate friends.

As I enter His presence daily through prayer, I experience peace, boldness, rest, good stewardship, and fearlessness. All the benefits of God and the Fruit of the Spirit manifest as I yield to the Holy Spirit by walking in the Spirit and not fulfilling the lust of the flesh.

As I enter the Lord's presence daily, I receive a Fresh Fire Anointing; I experience God's glorious, wondrous, excellent Presence.

Hebrews 10:19 tells us that we can confidently enter the Most Holy Place by the blood of Jesus. Because of the Blood of Jesus, we can now enter God's presence boldly by this new and living way He has made for us. When we boldly enter God's presence, we find everything we need for life and Godliness. The Bible says in Heb 4:16 that we can come boldly into the throne of grace to obtain mercy and find grace to help in times of need.

If you are unsatisfied with your life and how things are going, I invite you to enter God's presence, seek His Face, become intimately acquainted with him, and get to know and recognize His voice so He can lead and guide you into all truths. I guarantee your life will never be the same.

Entering the Presence of God is just like the air you breathe. The song says, "This is the air I breathe, your Holy Presence living in me, and I am lost without you. You realize you're lost without Him because in Him you Live and Move and Have Your Being. The song continues to say, "I am desperate for you. When you are desperate for Him, you intensely desire to know Him. You hunger and thirst after righteousness; you seek first the Kingdom of God and His righteousness; you want to know Him better."

It's time to seek His Presence, to seek His Face. Why? Because there is power in the Presence of God, there is healing in His Presence, and you become increasingly acquainted with Him when you seek His Face by getting into His Presence.

So, begin to Thank Him, begin to Praise Him, Get into His Word and let His Word get into you, pray – talk to God and watch God move you from FAITH TO FAITH, VICTORY TO VICTORY, AND GLORY TO GLORY! God Bless You!

Saundra Yvonne Werts

ABOUT THE AUTHOR

Saundra Yvonne Werts

Werts Ministries—Werts Ministries teaches and preaches about an available and accessible God whose love can reach you no matter where you are.

Saundra Werts, also known as Lady Werts, is a native of New Jersey. She is married to Bishop Arthur N. Werts, Pastor of Second Baptist Church in Ruther Glen, Virginia, and Presiding Bishop of The Missionary Church International (TMCI).

They have two married children and five grand blessings. Lady Werts is an ordained minister who assists her husband in several ministry areas. She has completed several biblical studies and is enrolled in Andersonville Theological Seminary.

And be Ye Transformed...

Psalm 119: Presence - "I will delight in your statutes; I will not forget your word."

PASTOR DE'RAIN F. IRVIN

IN HIS PRESENCE

Totally Transformed

WHO DROPPED YOU AND MADE YOU LAME?

Pastor De'Rain F. Irvin

Have you ever asked God, "Are you listening?" Or have you ever wondered if His Word would ever be manifested in your life? Feelings of rejection and not being loved caused me to think that I didn't deserve it and wouldn't receive it. But that devil is a liar!

I have scriptures that I quote for encouragement. We all do. One is, "For I know the plans I have for you," declares the Lord, "plans to prosper you and not to harm you, plans to give you hope and a future." Jeremiah 29:11. I must be transparent; I often didn't feel like I had hope or that I would have the future I longed for.

Throughout my life, there have been many men who have dropped me and made me lame. Men who were supposed to and promised to love, honor, encourage, and protect me did the opposite. I have cried out through the hurt and tears, "God, when is it my turn!"

The most devastating drop came early in life. My father dropped me and made me lame! The damage that he did consumed me most of my life. It made me vulnerable to other men who had the same sorry characteristics, the Daddy Complex! I looked for validation and protection from men.

Like many good women, I was mistreated, hurt, emotionally abused, and misunderstood by men who promised to love and honor me. I was never physically abused! I'll tell you that tragic story another time.

I have been divorced, delivered as I say, twice. The second man in my life to drop me and make me lame was my first husband. ....No comment!

I genuinely thought my second husband was a gift from God. After ten years, he abandoned me. Under the disguise of taking his mother home to WV, he never came back. He was the third man to drop me and make me lame. Lord, I've had enough!

A fourth man in my life dropped me and made me lame. Ironically, he doesn't even know it. He also did not know it was the worst time of my life. It was during the same time that my husband abandoned me. He was my superintendent.

I was blessed to open a new school named after an influential African American educator, Fannie W. Fitzgerald. She was among the "Courageous Four," the first African American women to integrate into white schools in that school system. We implemented many programs, tutored students, and provided additional support; however, we missed the mark for three years.

A principal's job is not secured by what she knows or even by what she does. It is secured by how students score on state standardized tests. They have the No Child Left Behind Act, but what about the No Principal Left Behind Act?

My assistant superintendent shared an anonymous survey. It stated I hold faculty meetings to scream and cuss out the staff. It was ironic because I don't yell and never use profanity! Can you imagine someone holding something against you from an anonymous survey, and you can't defend yourself?

I was upset with God. I gave God my resume of what I had done for Him, and I didn't understand why He was allowing these heathen principals to be successful and not me, who was faithfully serving Him. Two men dropped me simultaneously: my husband and my superintendent. My thought, God, you got some serious explaining to do!

I had a meeting with the deputy superintendent. God allowed me to hold my peace as she was downright nasty. I looked at that woman and said, "There is nothing you can say or do to make me act unGodly or unladylike. She said, "We don't have a job for you." I said, "OK, but my God will provide. Five minutes after the meeting, she found me a position. My God will supply my every need!

Whenever I saw her, she said, "I want to commend you for handling that situation with class and dignity." My inward response was, but you didn't. My students met the state standards for their SOL tests! Thank you, God, for answering my prayer and letting me go out on top!

During this most difficult, humiliating, and embarrassing period in my life, I heard the enemy telling me to take my life. I had to rebuke that spirit of suicide repeatedly, and I didn't tell anyone. I was embarrassed. Please don't suffer in silence! Reach out to another Sistah or your Pastor! You are not alone! Tell somebody!!

Glory to God for my redemption! These last 12 years of my educational career at Beville Middle School were the most fulfilling experiences of my career. My principal, Tim Keenan, and assistant principal, Victor Garcia, were a blessing. These two men restored my faith in men because they unwaveringly supported, protected, encouraged, and appreciated me. They showed me how real men love their wives and their family! I genuinely admire and appreciate them for restoring my faith in men.

The tragedy of COVID-19 in 2020 impacted the world, especially Christians. Prayer became our love language. COVID-19 taught me to bask In His Presence through prayer, worship, and praise by developing a more intimate relationship with Jesus.

On July 18, 2020, my son was attending a class at church. As the class was ending, a deranged man entered and attacked the Pastor. My son intervened, saving the Pastor's life, who was stabbed in the chest. My son was stabbed twice. I will let them tell their story @ http://www.youtube.com/@ANewThang-v1r.

God demanded me to pray and intercede on behalf of the Pastor, whom I didn't know. Through interceding for the Pastor's healing, the person I didn't know, God manifested the healing of the person I did know. Through obedience, I learned to bask In His Presence during intercessory prayer. When you intercede on behalf of others, your unselfishness will bring great rewards and blessings. If you don't believe me, I dare you to try it!

In September 2020, we began to study the book Kingdom Strong: The Making of Kingdom Warriors by Prophetess Monica Ollivierre. It was through this book study that I developed my daily spiritual workout. On December 8, 2020, God sent a prophetic word to me through Prophetess Ollivierre: Some things in your life have been dropped, and you have been dropped. As a result, just like Mephibosheth, some wrong mindsets about yourself have developed. He was a prince living as a pauper. You are a king. I speak to the King inside you and say, rise. Rise to the place that I have called you to. Rise to your rightful place. Your rightful place is found in My Word. Study Mephibosheth, which will show you who you were, who you are, and where I am taking you. ......for Mephibosheth, said the King, he shall eat at my table, as one of the King's sons." 2 Samuel 9:11 KJV. I received it, believed it, and walked in it!

My father passed away many years ago. In 2023, early in the morning, I heard God say, "Forgive him." I wrote in my journal and cried out, Daddy, I forgive you! I was set free.

God healed, restored, and elevated me. God birthed (1) 3N1MINISTRIES, LLC., a validation station! (2) My book, I Am Royalty! I Am Who God Says I Am – A journal of my journey to affirmations, confirmations, edifications, and transformations of who God says I am. (3) YouTube channels: A New Thang! 60 Seconds to Live By with Minister DIVA and (4). Brickhozz, Inc., which will be my parent company!

Like Mephibosheth, I sit at the King's table daily to bask In His Presence!! To God Be the Glory!!

Pastor De'Rain F. Irvin

GET & STAY CONNECTED:
Website: www.3n1min.com
E-Mail: 3n1min@gmail.com
FB: www.facebook.com/DerainIrvin
IG: www.instagram.com/derainirvin
Linkedin: www.linkedin.com/in/pastor-de-rain-irvin-277154134

YouTube: 60 Seconds to Live by with Minister DIVA - - www.youtube.com/@60SecondstoLiveByWithMinis-z5n

YouTube: A New Thang with Pastor De'Rain F. Irvin- www.youtube.com/@ANewThang-v1r

ABOUT THE AUTHOR

Pastor De'Rain F. Irvin

CEO - 3N1 MINISTRIES, LLC.
CEO - Minister DIVA, and Coach "D"

Pastor De'Rain F. Irvin was born and raised in South Philadelphia. She is a proud mother, grandmother, and great-grandmother. She is the Executive Pastor of Hope Aglow Empowerment Church in Northern Virginia.

Pastor Irvin retired as an educator after 41 years. She graduated from Regent University -M. Ed., Education Administration/Leadership and Cheyney University - B.S.-Special Education, Mentally/Physically Handicapped. She is currently a doctoral student at Andersonville Theological Seminary.

At age 60, God birthed a CEO - 3N1MINISTRIES, LLC.:
(1) Pastor De'Rain F. Irvin – Minister
(2) Minister DIVA – Christian Comedian
(3) Coach "D" – John Maxwell, certified speaker/trainer/coach/teacher

At age 62, God birthed an Author: I Am Royalty! I Am Who God Says I Am!

At age 64, God birthed a change in thinking: Behold, God is doing A New Thing!"

Pastor Irvin's mission is simple yet profound in the lives of those who will be impacted. God has placed in her a calling, a desire, and a determination to be an encourager and exhorter of women.

Her genuine heart desires to empower people to overcome emotional, mental, social, spiritual, educational, economic, and technological barriers to maximize their fullest potential and become all that the Word of God says they can be.

Pastor De'Rain F. Irvin is a Woman of God who desires to be used for the Glory of God!!

And be Ye Transformed...

Psalm 103: Bless the Lord, O my soul: and all that is within me, bless his holy name. Bless the Lord, O my soul, and forget not all his benefits:

REV. WILLIAM FELLS, JR.

IN HIS PRESENCE

Totally Transformed

GOD'S BENEFIT PACKAGE: THE BEST ON EARTH

By Reverend William Fells, Jr.

Welcome, and thank you for joining us today! I'm delighted to introduce you to an extraordinary benefits package offered by Jesus Christ Incorporated, a company with unparalleled offerings that transcend anything you've ever encountered. At Jesus Christ Incorporated, we pride ourselves on providing the universe's most comprehensive and life-transforming benefits. Let's dive into the specifics of this divine offer and explore why it stands unmatched.

A Benefits Package Beyond Compare

Imagine a valuable benefits package surpassing all earthly treasures—diamonds, rubies, or even monetary wealth. This is the kind of offer we're presenting to you today. The benefits package from Jesus Christ Incorporated includes full medical, dental, and vision care and an everlasting life insurance policy extending beyond this lifetime. It is truly a package of eternal significance.

The Wisdom of Psalm 103

To understand the depth of this package, let's turn to Psalm 103 to see some incredible benefits our divine leader provides. The Psalm begins with a call to bless the Lord and remember His benefits, highlighting how God cares for those who follow Him. Here's a closer look:

• Forgiveness of Sins: The package starts with the assurance that all your sins are forgiven. This profound gift demonstrates God's radical love and willingness to cleanse you from all past transgressions. According to Romans 3:23, everyone has sinned, but God's forgiveness through Jesus Christ is complete and absolute, ensuring nothing can separate you from His love (Romans 8:38-39).

• Healing: God's benefits include physical, spiritual, and emotional healing. This package promises restoration and renewal, with Jesus offering healing and eternal life. John 10:10 reminds us that Jesus came to provide life abundantly, ensuring your well-being is cared for in every aspect.

• Redemption: The reality of human sin is that it brings death, but the gift of God is eternal life through Christ Jesus (Romans 6:23). Jesus' sacrifice paid the price for our sins, offering redemption and saving us from everlasting destruction. His resurrection secures an eternal future for all who accept this gift.

• Love and Compassion: God's love and compassion are infinite. His actions embody the essence of love described in 1 Corinthians 13:4-8—love that is patient, kind, and enduring. This divine love is a benefit and a guarantee that God's support will never fail you.

• Provision: As our Jehovah Jireh, God is our provider. Every good thing comes from Him, and He promises to meet our needs and bless us abundantly. This provision ensures that our lives are filled with satisfaction and joy, reflecting the overflowing blessings God has for us.

Additional Complimentary Benefits

In addition to the core benefits, there are several complimentary perks included in your package:

• Access to the Holy Spirit: Available in John 14:16, this benefit provides guidance, comfort, and support.

• Peace, Joy, and Hope: Promised in John 14:27 and Romans 15:13, these gifts enhance your emotional and spiritual well-being.

• The Full Armor of God: Detailed in Ephesians 6:11-13, this universal security system offers protection against life's challenges.

• Ever-Present Help: As described in Matthew 28:20, God promises to be with you in every circumstance.

Are you ready to accept this extraordinary offer and become a representative of Jesus Christ Incorporated? This choice promises not only eternal life, but a life filled with unparalleled blessings and support. The offer stands open—embrace it and experience a transformation that transcends the ordinary.

Reverend William Fells, Jr.

ABOUT THE AUTHOR

Reverend William Fells, Jr.

Hello, I'm William Fells Jr., a minister, entrepreneur, author, mentor, and dedicated family man. I am passionate about building faith in all areas of life.

My journey has taught me to activate faith beyond current circumstances, and I strive to inspire others to do the same.

As the best-selling book says, faith is the substance of things hoped for and the evidence of things not seen.

GET & STAY CONNECTED @

Email: Eyeontheprize85@gmail.com
FB: www.facebook.com/WillFells?mibextid=ZbWKwL
IG: @Youweremadeforthis_

And be Ye Transformed...

Isaiah 43:2 - "When you pass through the waters, I will be with you; and through the rivers, they shall not overwhelm you; when you walk through fire you shall not be burned, and the flame shall not consume you."

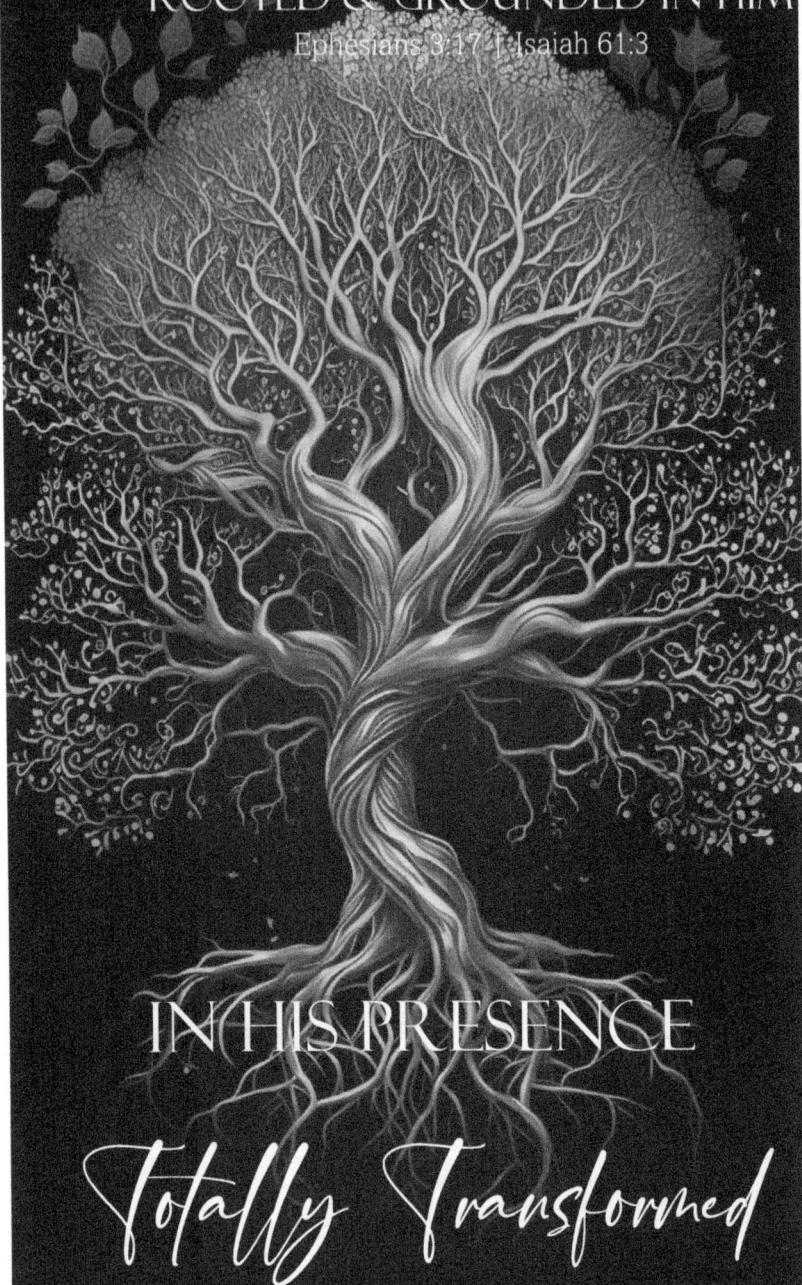